blin and Cork
le of Two Cities

Tom Cronin

Published by Tom Cronin

First published 2017
© Tom Cronin 2017
The rights of Tom Cronin to be identified as the author of this work have been
asserted by him in accordance with the Copyright, Designs and Patents Act of 1988.

ISBN 978-1-78222-467-9

Printed by CPI Group (UK) Ltd, Croydon, CR0 4YY

TABLE OF CONTENTS

FOREWORD

This book had not been planned it sort of fell into place. For a number of years I had it in my mind to do something about Dublin and Cork. I had a lot of material about all of the bridges in both cities. I believe I was the first to record all of the Dublin bridges. When I went looking for information some had been recorded but most had not. I had some rare photographs of both Cork and Dublin taken in the 1960's. However when I stumbled across some very rare photos taken around 1875. It seems that an Irish emigrant living in Chicago sent a team to Ireland to record the mood and take some wonderful photographs. Just as interesting as the photographs is the text it allows us to gauge the mind-set of the people at the time, you must remember that this was barely twenty five years after the famine and it gives us an invaluable look back at this time in history.

I hope that you enjoy this modest attempt at recording a tiny piece of our Irish history.

Tom Cronin.

ACKNOWLEDGEMENTS

Irish Examiner
Irish National Museum
R.S. McGowan
J.F. Finerty

BANK OF IRELAND, FORMERLY PARLIAMENT HOUSE, DUBLIN. – No person of Irish race can look upon the splendid structure shown in the sketch and which stands on the north side of College Green, without a mingled feeling of pride and sorrow – pride in the glory of its architecture and sorrow for the national tragedy which, in 1801, degraded the Irish Houses of Parliament from their high estate, and subsequently made them the offices of the National Bank of Ireland. "Did public virtue cease to animate the people, " exclaimed Thomas Francis Meagher, the great Irish orator and subsequent American general, in 1847, "the Senate House, which, even in its desecrated state, lends an Italian glory to this metropolis, would forbid it to expire!" Although the most classical public building in Europe, without any exception, nobody knows who was the original architect, and, in fact, the history of its construction is wrapped in more or less mystery. It was begun under the administration of Lord Carteret in 1729, and, in 1785, a portico, with Corinthian columns, was added to the entrance of the House of Lords. As the other columns are the Ionic order, the effect is incongruous, but most noble façade on College Green, having an extent 147 feet, redeems every defect of detail. In the days of Ireland's independence, the eloquence of Grattan, Flood, Carran and Hussey Burgh, poured forth in the Irish House of Commons, rivalled that of the Greek and Roman masters. Although used solely for banking purposes, the building has been but little altered since1802, when the Directors of the Bank of Ireland purchased it from the government for 200,000 and a nominal yearly rental.

SHANDON CHURCH, CORK CITY.- Although not particularly ancient, the church of St. Anne Shandon, has, because of that sweet singer, the Rev. Francis Mahony, much more widely known as "Father Prout," acquired a popularity equal to that of any sacred edifice in Ireland. The original structure was destroyed by fire and the building shown in the sketch was begun in 1722. The steeple, one hundred and twenty feet high is out of all proportion to the size of the church but possesses a magnificent peal of bells. The name Shandon – in Gaelic written Scandun – means "Old Fort". Father Mahony thought it the brightest spot on earth, and when he died in Paris, in 1866, friends conveyed his remains to Cork, where they were buried in Shandon churchyard. He had heard –

Bells tolling old "Adrian's Mole" in,
Their thunder rolling from the Vatican
And Cymbals glorious swinging uproarious
In the gorgeous turrets of Notre Dame.

But thy sounds were sweeter than
the Dome of Peter
Fling's o'er the Tiber, pealing solemnly –
Oh, the bells of Shandon sound far more grand on
The pleasant waters of the River Lee!

VIEW IN MITCHELSTOWN, COUNTY CORK.

This well-known place is the north-eastern corner of the County of Cork, not far from Funcheon River, and near where Limerick and Tipperary approach the Cork boundary line. It is the centre of a fine agricultural district, does a good internal trade, and has about 2,500 inhabitants. This section of Munster has always been intensely patriotic. Only a few miles distant in Tipperary, is Killbehenny, where the famous Colonel John O'Mahony, the founder of the Fenian Brotherhood, was born, and whence he "took the hills", as armed "rebel," in the fall of 1848 – a movement that compelled his departure from Ireland to France, and thence to this country, where he was, for many years, a formidable thorn in the side of the British governments. He died in New York, neglected and impoverished, after a life of toil in the cause of Irish independence, about twenty years ago. His pride was such that he would not let those who would have gladly aided him know his distress. Mitchelstown won a recent celebrity as the focus of the Land League movement in Cork. Only a few years since, at a meeting held in the market place, the police causelessly fired on people, killing three poor farmers and wounding many others. "Remember Mitchelstown!" is still a rallying cry among the political admirers of Charles Stewart Parnell.

KINGSBRIDGE TERMINUS, DUBLIN.

Dublin, metropolitan in every feature, boasts many fine railroad structures, but none more graceful and commodious than the fine building pictured in the above sketch. It stands on the right bank of the Liffey, at Kingsbridge, a structure built in 1827, and named after the most unworthy George IV, in commemoration of this visit to Dublin six years before. It is the terminus of the Great Southern and Western Railway lines, which traverse most of the southern, eastern and western portions of Ireland. Kingsbridge station offers every possible accommodation to travellers. It has good restaurants and excellent attendance. The porters handle baggage with dexterity of their American brethren, but with considerable more care of the contents of trunks and "boxes" than our world-renowned baggage smashers. During the Fenian troubles of 1865-7, the Irish revolutionists and Scotland Yard detectives played hide and seek with each other around this station several times. Among the "suspects" of the period was Captain John A. Geary, of Lexington, Ky., one of Stonewell Jackson's men. His military bearing attracted the "lynx-eye" of a "sleuth". He approached the Captain, who pointing to his own trunk, said "break it open at once!" The "bobby", completely deceived, did as ordered. Geary jumped on the moving train, made his way to Limerick, vanquished there a constable who sought to arrest him, and escaped to America.

EXTERIOR VIEW, CHRIST CHURCH CATHEDRAL, DUBLIN.- Above is given an exterior view of the venerable Christ Church Cathedral, which is regarded by most antiquarians as by far the most interesting of all Dublin churches.

Originally it is said to have been built by Christianised Danes, about the 11th century; it was rebuilt by Anglo-Normans, who on establishing themselves in the metropolis, constituted the church a cathedral of the Pale. In the general type of its architecture it differs from most Irish churches, as almost everything approaching the Romanesque has been eliminated from its construction. Race prejudice was indulged in to such an extent that, towards the end of the 14th century, a law prohibiting native Irishmen from professing themselves in the sanctuary was passed and carried into effect. This held good, except during the brief region of James 11, and the eighteenth century had almost passed into history before an Irish-born man was admitted, even as Vicar-choral, in this exclusive and bigoted church. It was frequently all but destroyed by fire and other visitations and was subjected to many changes, from its foundation by Sitric the Dane, for secular canons, in 1038, down to the reign of Elizabeth. It was on Easter Sunday, A.D. 1551 that the Liturgy was first read in English, as far as Ireland was concerned in Christ Church. This was the signal for the long series of wars that may be described as religio-national,which terminated in 1603 with the surrender of the Ulster Catholic Princes. Christ Church was fully restored, by the liberality of Henry Roe, and under direction of George Street, R. A., in 1871-8.

STRONGBOW'S MONUMENT, CHRIST CHURCH, DUBLIN.

Richard de Clare, Earl of Pembroke, nicknamed, "Strongbow," because of his strength and skill in archery, was the chief and most accomplished, of the band of Norman adventurers that invaded Ireland on the invitation of Dermod MacMurrough, the traitor Kind of Leinster, during the years 1169-72. MacMurrough eloped with the wife of O'Ruarc, Prince of Breffni, during the latter's absence on a pious pilgrimage. This led to the adulterer's flight from Ireland, and the subsequent fatal invasion of the Normans. The poet Moore has immortalized the episode in his well-known ballad, "The Valley Lay Smiling before Me." Strongbow after making nominal conquest of Leinster, married Eva, the heiress of MacMurrough, and laid claim to a large portion of Irish territory, which he held with the strong hand. This great Norman chief was as politic as brave, for, says his biographer, Cambrensis, "what he could not effect by force, he accomplished by soft words and fair promises. He died not many years after the invasion and was interred in Christ Church, which he aided in restoring. The roof fell in and wrecked the original monument during the fifteenth century, but the latter was re-erected by Sir Henry Sydney, Lord Deputy, during the reign of Elizabeth. The full length effigy shown in the sketch is alleged to be that of Strongbow.

HOTEL PARK, QUEENSTOWN, CO. CORK. - All flunkies are disgusting but none more so than the Irish specimen of that ignoble tribe. He is living libel on an impetuous and high-spirted race that, whatever its temperamental faults – the common heritage of humanity – has never, as a body, forgotten its self-respect. Were the rule of Great Britain and Ireland, even ordinarily friendly to the latter country, there might be some weak excuse for outward manifestations of selfinterested "loyalty," but it is notorious that Queen Victoria is positively antagonistic to Ireland and the Irish. Yet, in Dublin and other Irish cities, it is not unusual to see such signs over shops as "William Jenkins, chiropodist-extraordinary to the Queen;" "John Jones, chimney sweeper, by appointment, to her Majesty" and other trade legends equally exaggerated and absurd. The Queen of England, in all probability never "darkened the doors," of the "Queen's Hotel" at Queenstown – the pretty park of which, overlooking the harbour, is shown in the picture. But the poor old "Cove of Cork" had an epidemic of flunkeyism fifty years ago when it changed its name, not for the better, and its whole career has been coloured by Victoria's flying visit before she became "the widow" of Rudyard Kipling's barrack room tales and songs. "The Queen's" is, however, the leading hostelry in Queenstown, and is much patronized by American travellers. Its situation is simply delightful and it commands a splendid view of Ireland's most noted seaport.

THE WELLINGTON TESTIMONIAL, PHOENIX PARK. – This ponderous shaft is the most striking feature among the monuments of Dublin's spacious pleasure ground. The obelisk is constructed of Wicklow granite, and the bronze panels in the column, which is approached by a flight of steps, are composed of molten metal of cannon captured during Wellington's immortal campaigns. These bear, besides representations of many famous scenes of conflict, the names of his numerous splendid victories.

The total height of the monument is 205 feet, and the general effect is massive and angular, like the character of the "Iron Duke" – rather than symmetrical and graceful.

It was built as a result of "popular subscription" – mainly confined to the "nobility and gentry" – in 1817, while yet the glory of Waterloo was fresh in the public mind. Dublin claims the Duke as her son – fixing his birthplace in Upper Merrion Street, instead of at Dangan Castle, County Meath, which long held undivided claim to that distinction.

The Duke, whose greatness seemed to terminate with the battlefield, was an inveterate Tory, and never called himself and Irishman, although his family, on both sides, had been settled in Ireland for centuries before his birth, in 1769. Consequently, his memory is not revered by a majority of his fellow-countrymen, who, however, respect his martial record.

THE GRATTAN STATUE, COLLEGE GREEN. – In 1876, the corporation of Dublin caused Foley's striking statue of Henry Grattan, the greatest of not alone Irish, but also of European, orators, of modern times, to be erected in College Green, opposite the old House of Parliament, in which he uttered the splendid speeches that have made his name immortal. Grattan, unlike O'Connell, was noted for vehemence and what may be called angularity of gesture. In fact, he was not what is termed a graceful speaker, but his language was sublime, and he had a magical influence over his audience. He could not move the masses of people, like the great Catholic Emancipator, but before the most critical parliamentary body in the world, as was the Irish House of Commons, he stood unrivalled. The artist represents him moving his famous Declaration of Irish Rights, April 19, 1780, in supporting which he said: "I never will be satisfied so long as the meanest cottager in Ireland has a link of the British chain clanking to his rags. He may be naked, he shall not be in irons. And I do see the time is at hand, the spirit is gone forth, the declaration is planted; and though great men should apostatize, yet the cause will live, and though the public speaker should yet the immortal fire shall outlast the organ which conveyed it, and the breath of liberty, like the word of the holy man, will not die with the prophet, but survive him."

MONKSTOWN, CO. CORK. – Among the many pretty villages that stud the emerald shores of the estuary of the river Lee is Monkstown, sketched above. It stands on the right bank of the river, in the midst of scenery that it is no exaggeration to call enchanting. "Glorious woods and teeming soil" characterize the whole neighbourhood of this delightful place. It possess, among other objects of interest, an old castle, now a ruin, which was built in 1636 under what Prof. Addey, in "Picturesque Ireland", calls "peculiar circumstances". The tradition runs that during the absence of the owner of the demesne, who was serving in the army of Philip of Spain, his wife, whose name as Anastasia, resolved to pleasing surprise him by building a quadrangular castle without diminishing his exchequer. In order to achieve this end, she compelled the tenants on the estate to purchase from her the groceries and other necessities of existence, consumed or worn by them, at an advance on the prices at which she was enabled to buy goods wholesale. A keen woman of business, she succeeded admirably, for when the balance was finally struck, it was found that the completed edifice had cost only four pence – commonly called a "groat" – in excess of the receipts from the sales of merchandise. This castle fell into decay during the Williamite wars.

THE SCOTS GUARDS, DUBLIN. – The Sketch represents a "relief" of the Scots Fusilier Guards, commonly called the 3rd Foot Guards of the British army, marching to their post in the Irish capital. At the head march three stalwart Highland pipers, who make the ancient streets ring with the weird music of "the plaided Gael." The Scots Guards have not been much in Ireland, but they are more popular in Dublin than either the Grenadiers or the Coldstreams. The latter, in particular, made themselves obnoxious to people, and several bloody fights marked their stay in the metropolis. The Scotch troops, in general, are well conducted, and as they are mainly Celts, they really fraternize with the impulsive and good natured Dubliners, who however, regard all British troops with very natural distrust. These Guards are a striking body of men, tall and stalwart, with flaming scarlet coats and immense bear-skin caps. They have a good record as fighters, particularly in the Waterloo and Crimean campaigns. At Hourgomont, they aided in repelling the fierce attach of the corps of Prince Jerome Bonaparte on the chateau, which was the key to the British position. They lost heavily in officers and enlisted men. At the Alma, in 1854, they were particularly distinguished. Like the other Household regiments, they are always liable to be sent on Foreign Service, but are rarely called upon, unless in cases of grave emergency.

ST. LUKE'S CHURCH, CORK. – The foregoing sketch represents St. Luke's Episcopalian Church, situated on an elevation of the city called by some Napoleonic, worshippers, "Montenotte." The site overlooks the northern end of the southern capital and the sylvan valley of the Lee. It is not a very large edifice and is designed in the perpendicular Gothic style, often called the Scholastic Gothic, of the 15th century, but is a very handsome specimen of that school of architecture. The material used in its exterior construction is of a soft, grey limestone, quarried in the neighbourhood. It has a pinnacle tower and a spire of cut stone. St. Luke's is not an ancient edifice. It was built during the first quarter of this century, after the design of George Richard Paine, the same architect who made the plans of Blackrock Castle, a picturesque land mark on the west bank of the fine river. Mr Paine was also the architect of the handsome Cork branch of the Bank of Ireland, and of many of the stately mansions that are reflected in the clear waters of the Lee. One of the most noted residences designed by him is the mansion of Woodville, the seat of the Penrose family, in which Washington Irving laid the scene in the life of Sarah Curran, fiancée of Robert Emmet, sketched in "The Broken Heart." It is one of the most delightful spots in Ireland.

PARNELL MEMORIAL PROCESSION, DUBLIN. – It has been custom of the political followers of the late Charles Stewart Parnell, headed by John E. Redmond, M. P., to organize a memorial procession on each anniversary of his death, which occurred on October 7th, 1981. The sketch shows the head of the column proceeding to Glasnevin Cemetery, where the remains of the great Irish leader are interred, over the superb O'Connell Bridge, while throngs of people stand respectfully on each side of the paraders, as they slowly march on their mournful pilgrimage to the flower-covered grave of the immortal patriot. Behind the carriages tramp in solid array the National Societies and organized Trades of Dublin., who always present a fine appearance. Following these come the various delegations from the country, rank on rank. Every organization is preceded by a band, playing airs appropriate to the occasion. Dublin has always been famous for its funeral parades – the most notable having been those of O'Connell, Terence Bellew MacManus, the Manchester Martyrs – a mock funeral, because they were buried in quicklime in Salford prison, England – and that of Parnell himself. At the MacManus funeral, in November, 1861 several Irish soldiers of the Dublin garrison joined in the procession, and uncovered their heads, like the rest, when they passed the theatre of Robert Emmet's execution. Those men were sent immediately "on foreign service."

O'CONNELL MONUMENT, DUBLIN. – This splendid national tribute to the Emancipator of the Irish Catholics, stands at the northern end of O'Connell (formerly Carlisle) Bridge, and is after the design of the late J. H. Foley, the most widely known, perhaps of modern Irish sculptors. Mr. Foley died before the work was completed, but his model has been faithfully followed. The statue represents the Irish Demosthenes, pleading for liberty of this country, before a "monster meeting" of the Irish people. The capacious chest is expanded; the cloak, or mantle – as well remembered in Ireland as Napoleon's grey overcoat in France – thrown back from the broad shoulders, and the handsome, massive head proudly raised in haughty defiance of the national enemy. It, in short, pictures O'Connell as he appeared in the zenith of his power and fame, "when sitting sole on Tara's Hill there hung a million on his will!" The back of the effigy is turned, as if in aversion, upon the Nelson monument, which stands near the opposite end of O'Connell (formerly Sackville) street, while the steady gaze is directed toward the point where stand the ancient Irish houses of parliament, now occupied by the Bank of Ireland, on historic College Green. The mobile lips of the majestic figure seem to say, as once said the orator himself – "I am now an old man, and may go to the grave leaving my dearest hope – the independence of Ireland – unfulfilled, but, when I am dead, another generation, with redder blood in their veins, will arise to burst the chains of my country."

WHERE ROBERT EMMET DIED, DUBLIN. – It was Tuesday, Sept, 20, 1803, about noon, that Robert Emmet, the young, gallant and unselfish Irish patriot was executed for the "rising" of July 23, in the same year. "in Thomas Street, at the end of Bridgefoot Street, and nearly opposite St. Catherine's church" – the edifice shown in the sketch. Dr. R. R. Madden, M.R.I.A., author of the Lives of Robert and Thomas Addis Emmet, and of the United Irishmen, is our authority. Emmet was only twenty-five years old when he perished on this fatal spot, and his execution in thus described by the historian: "The scaffold was a temporary one, formed by laying boards across a number of empty barrels that were placed, for this purpose, nearly in the middle of the street. Through this platform rose two posts, 12 feet high, and a transverse beam was placed across them. Underneath this beam, about three feet from the platform, was a single narrow plank, supported on two slight ledges, on which the prisoner was to stand at the moment of execution." The platform was reached by a ladder. Emmet mounted the scaffold quickly, and said in a sonorous voice: "My friends! I die in peace and with sentiments of universal love and kindness toward all men." In a moment the rope was adjusted, the cap drawn down, the plank tilted and brave Robert Emmet, Catholic Ireland's Protestant patriot-hero, was a corpse! The hangman immediately served the head from the body and, holding it up before the horrified people, shouted: "This is the head of a traitor!" Ireland's worship of the martyr's memory gives the live to the official butcher.

THE CUSTOM HOUSE, DUBLIN.- Nothing so fills an Irishman of spirit with indignation, on visiting the widowed capital of his country, as to behold her grand public buildings almost deserted, and in some instances falling into decay. One of the finest monuments of Irish architectural genius in the last century, is the Custom House, situated on Eden Quay, on the north bank of the Liffey. It was begun, after the design of James Gandon, in 1781 and was completed ten years later. The structure forms a quadrangle of 375 by 209 feet. It has four fronts of different design and is "composed of pavilions at each end, joined by arcades and united in the centre." The pavilions terminate with the arms of Ireland and the facades are embellished with exquisite taste. Many fine allegorical figures add to the beauty of the design. The dome, which is of majestic appearance rises to a height of 125 feet while a state of Hope, 16 feet high, placed on a massive pedestal, and resting on an anchor, gives dramatic effect to the whole. Since the fatal "Union," only a portion of the building is used for custom purposes. The remainder is devoted to the use of public departments, such as the Board of Works and the Poor Law Commission.

THE CITY HALL, DUBLIN. – The above splendid public building was erected after the design of the great Dublin architect of the last century, Thomas Cooley, in 1769. Dr. Charles Lucas, the famous Irish patriot, who preceded Flood and Grattan in public favour, secured the purchase money for the site from the Irish parliament. The money for the structure was raised under a lottery system and by subscription. The edifice was originally called the Royal Exchange, but seems to have been very little used for purposes of trade and finance. It became, however, a favourite meeting place of the people of Dublin, and its fine all, Daniel O'Connell in the year 1800, made his speech in public on the Irish question. In 1852, the Royal Exchange became the City Hall of Dublin. Here the mayor has his office and the aldermen their place of assembly. The principal front, on Parliament Street consists of imposing portico, with pediment supported by Corinthian columns. The western front, on Castle Street, has a portico of four Corinthian pillars, but without a pediment. The entablature around the structure is continuous, and there is also artistic balustrade around the top, except where the pediment interrupts its course. The hall contains statues of O'Connell and Drummond by Hogan – the former a remarkably fine work of art. The statue of Grattan, by Chantrey, is considered excellent of the patriot, and there are many other effigies of historical interest.

BERMINGHAM TOWER, DUBLIN CASTLE. – The foregoing picture represents the Bermingham Tower, of Dublin Castle, which was partially rebuilt in 1810, and is about the only part of the fortress, begun by Meyler Fitzhenry, Norman Lord Justice in 1205, and completed by Archbishop Henri De Loundres, in 1220, that may be considered original. Time and change have done away with the rest of the ancient stronghold, which has been replaced by modern, rambling structures of no historical importance. The castle has been the malodorous seat of English government in Ireland for more than three hundred years. Since 1560, in the reign of Elizabeth, it has been residence of the English Lords Lieutenant, and has been the theatre of many black crimes committed against the Irish. In its dungeons, chiefs have been cruelly imprisoned, and in its councils innumerable plots against the liberty of Ireland have been hatched. The name of "The Castle", is as hateful to most Irish ears, as the Bastille was to the French. It became particularly infamous during the '98 troubles, chiefly because of the manufacture there of odious spies and villainous informers. Curran in his speech defending Peter Finery, accused of "treason to the Crown," denounced its as a catacomb in which "the wretch buried as a man, was dug up as a witness!" Many Irishmen, and Englishmen also, favour the abolition of the viceroyalty and "the castle", with it. Bermingham Tower is in the Lower Castle Yard, and it is therepository of the state records.

KING WILLIAM'S STATUE, DUBLIN. – The equestrian statue of William 111, stands in College Green, and has stood there, more or less since A.D. 1701. We say "more or less," because no statue in the world, perhaps has been subject to so many vicissitudes. It has been insulted, mutilated and blown up so many times, that the original figure, never particularly graceful, is now a battered wreck, pieced and patched together, like an old, worn-out garment. The material used in casting the effigy was lead, and, in consequence there was little difficulty in disfiguring it when the spirit of malice, or mischief, moved the anti-Orange populace of the Irish capital. King William was, however, the idol of the anti-national Protestants of Ireland, called the Orangemen, to distinguish them from the patriotic co-religionists – the followers of Grattan, Wolfe Tone and the Emmets. This element often fought vigorously in defence of the unfortunate memento of the Victor of the Boyne. Once, indeed in 1782 the patriotic Protestant Volunteers, who virtually won the parliamentary independence of Ireland for a time, assembled around the statue and pledged fealty to the cause of their country. Some years later they resolved to cease decorating the figure with orange ribbon on July 12 so as to avoid offense to their Catholic fellow-countrymen. The figures was last blown up in 1836, but was repaired, as shown in the sketch. Since that year it has been left in peace.

ANCIENT RUINS, CHRIST CHURCH, DUBLIN.

- No sacred edifice in all Europe, perhaps, has suffered more from fire than historic Christ Church in Dublin. Founded by Sitric the Dane, for Secular Canons, in 1038, it was changed more than a century later into a priory by St. Lawrence O'Tuhill, and underwent various alterations down to 1225. The wrathful native Irish, driven to desperation by Anglo-Norman tyranny, burned the outskirts of Dublin in 1283, the cathedral caught fire and the steeple, chapter house, cloisters and dormitory were consumed. A mass of debris covered the ground for generations, and some of the buildings were never restored, the steeple was, however, and was again burned in 1316. It is supposed that the remains shown in the picture are those of the original chapter house, as they bear all the marks of very ancient origin. Some antiquaries hold that they belong to the cloister, but all agree that they are the most interesting archaeological remains of ancient Dublin. A singular fact in connection with Christ Church cathedral is, that Lambert Simnel, one of the Yorkist pretenders to the English throne, was solemnly crowned here in 1486 as "Edward V1!" He found numerous followers among the Norman- Irish of the Pale, who also, to their ultimate ruin, followed the misfortunes of the other more brilliant "royal" adventurer, Perkin Warbeck, whom the King of Scotland recognised as "Richard IV."

IN THE MUSEUM, DUBLIN. – It has been a just complaint of Irishmen of talent that they have been handicapped, so to speak, in their pursuit of fame and fortune, unless they abandoned Irish subjects and curbed their national sentiments. Ireland has produced many painters and sculptors of note, but, like her chiefest soldiers, statesmen and authors they have been compelled, in general to devote their talent to the pleasing of other people than their own – in a word, to find a market for their talent outside of Ireland and Irish interests. The poverty and decay of public spirit in Ireland, justly attributed to the loss of national autonomy, has fixed this doom upon Irish genius. "Unprized are her sons till they learn to betray the principles of their sires. This is as true of the artists, Barry, Forde, Maclise, Foley and others, as of the soldiers, Wellington and Roberts, and authors and scientists like Leckey and Tyndall. Hogan, the only Irish sculptor who really devoted himself to Irish subjects, died in obscurity. Yet, although Ireland possess but a tithe of her children's works, Dublin is rich in an Art Gallery wherein are collected many of the finest studies of the great masters. The beautiful group of "The Mother," the creation of the sculptor I.H.Hall, R.S., speaks eloquently for itself as a masterpiece of its kind.

THE SHELBOURNE HOTEL, DUBLIN.

The Shelbourne, which stands on Stephens Green, although by no means the oldest, is, perhaps, the best known of the Dublin hotels, ranking with the Fifth Avenue, of New York and the Palmer of Chicago. It is, or at least used to be, the hostelry most affected by the Irish aristocrats, and the English visitors to the Emerald Isle. Mean of all parties met there on equal footing, and, indeed, there was a very little clashing in even the most violent eras of political excitement, for the clientele of the Shelbourne was, and is, overwhelming in favour of "things as they are." This is only natural, because its habitués generally possess "the fat of the land", while their less fortunate brethren – if, indeed, they admit the relationship of the untitled and unfortuned - have to be content with inferior accommodations. The Shelbourne, although patronized by the aristocracy, treats all corners with courtesy and hospitality. Gresham's, Morrisson's and other old-time hotels divide the public patronage with the Shelbourne, but the latter still holds the premier field in the Irish capital. It is a large and commodious building, modern in appearance and not possessed of any striking architectural features.

SHRINE AT GOUGANE BARRA, CO. CORK. – A typical Irish scene is presented to our readers in the foregoing picture. Amid the hoary ruins of the venerable shrine of St. Finn Barr, on the island in "lone Gougane Barra," the simple country people kneel and offer up their prayers to heaven as did their fathers before then for twelve hundred years! St. Finn Barr's natal day occurs on June 12, and each succeeding year, the peasantry, of both sexes, for miles on miles around the sacred spot, throng to the holy island and drink water from the pure depths of the blessed well, at which the patron saint, himself, slaked his thirst in the twilight dawn of Christianity that followed the black, repulsive night of Druidical paganism. The remains of the once stately ecclesiastical edifies are now but a feeble reminder of the splendour that crowned them in the early Christian ages of Ireland. It is singular that, in a land of piety, no effort has made to renovate them. At one time, the crowds that visited the ruins were not always free form turmoil, and a good priest, Farther O'Mahony, became resident of the island for the purpose of preserving order among the pilgrims.

His self-imposed task kept him a prisoner her from the year 1700 to 1728, when he died full of year, and in the odor of sanctity. His grave on the island is till pointed out to visitors.

A STREET IN QUEENSTOWN, CO. CORK. – When the flunkey corporation of the Cove of Cork changed the ancient designation of the picturesque place to Queenstown, in 1849, merely because of the female rule of England paid it a passing visit, the deposed officers proved the truth of the Prisoner of Chillon's statement "my very chains and I grew friends; to such a long communion tends." Queen Victoria carried nothing of value into the picturesque Cove but tool away its good name, which did not enrich her, but made the despoiled town poor indeed. It was many years before Ireland got accustomed to the new-fangled title of the favourite seaport. The town is situated on the south side of Great Island, in the magnificent harbour, and, owing to the character of the high ground, is built, amphitheatrically fashion, in tiers of streets, which gives it an odd and interesting appearance, from certain pints of view. The sketch shows one of the chief thoroughfares fronting on the harbour. Queenstown is fourteen miles from the City of Cork, and is an admiral's station for a British squadron. During the Napoleonic wars, thousands of troops embarked form the historic"Cove" for "the peninsula" and Belgium. The climates is very mild and equable, and this makes Queenstown a paradise for invalids. Most of the great American ocean liners stop at this port, which is the most prosperous in Ireland, except perhaps, Belfast. Many fine buildings adorn the town, and the new Catholic Cathedral is generally conceded to be the "finest of them all."

THE LIBRARY, TRINITY COLLEGE, DUBLIN. – This ancient and renowned institution of learning contains two libraries – the College and the Fagel. The former is one of the most valuable in the world, and contains more than 200,000 priceless volumes. It occupies a vast space, the whole side of a quadrangle, and its length is 270 feet. The main aisle, with its rows of busts, crowded shelves and lofty ceiling, is shown in the sketch. In this repository of knowledge some of the most eminent Irishmen of the last three centuries have been found inspiration for this great works in law, physics and literature. Goldsmith, Burke, Robert Emmet, Wolfe Tone, Thomas Davis, and many others celebrated in different walks of life, spent many delightful hours in this stately retreat of learned. James Clarence Manga, the Edgar Allan Poe of Ireland, was a constant visitor during his brilliant but troubled career, particularly to the Manuscript Room, which is unrivalled for the rarity and variety of the collection. The Fagel Library, which contains about 18,000 volumes, belonged to the family of that name in Holland, and was purchased for Trinity College about the end of the last century, its original owners having removed to England because of French invasion in 1794.

PATRICK STREET, CORK CITY. – What State Street is to Chicago, and Broadway to New York, Patrick Street is to the cheery southern metropolis of Ireland. It has a rival in the South Mall, but Patrick Street is ever dearer to the heart of the true Corkman, whether at home or "in climes beyond the sea." The famous thoroughfare has considerable of a crescent formation, and connects on the west with the Grand Parade – another imposing street which has somewhat of a history, as the place in which the "loyalists" of Cork once set upon an equestrian statue of George 11 of England – a monarch, by the way, who had never set foot in Ireland, and who is only remembered by the Irish people in connection with the victorious charge of the Franco-Irish Brigade on his son's column of 16,000 men, at the battle of Fontenoy. "Accursed" cried King George, referring to the penal enactments which drove the Catholic Irishmen form their country, "be the laws that deprive me of such soldiers!" Several years ago the statue disappeared one night, and was afterward found in the River Lee! Within recent years, a fine statue of Father Mathew, the renowned Irish apostle of temperance, who had in him the persuasive power of a St. Patrick, and whom Cork profoundly honours as a sage has been set up in Patrick Street and is an object of veneration to all beholders.

GUINNESS'S BREWERY, DUBLIN. – The virtues of "Dublin Stout" have been extolled by thousands of Americans who have travelled to Ireland. "Porter" - a species of dark complexioned ale – is to the Green Isle hat "lager" beer is to Germany. It is black-looking, foamy stuff, with a pungently bitter taste and great capability of intoxication, if copiously indulged in. Taken moderately, it is an excellent tonic and deserves to be called, rather than whiskey, which it has in a great measure supplanted, the national beverage of Ireland. "Guinness's Double X.," generally written, or printed "XX," enjoys almost a wide a reputation as, but far more democratic than, champagne, of which it is the liquid antithesis taste, colour, odor and effect. "Porter" is more of a sedative than an exhilarant to most constitutions. It is of ancient origin, but was brought to perfection by the Guinness experts early this century. The great brewery, pictured in the sketch, is situated on Guinness Wharf, lying along the Liffey. This wharf, during working hours always presents a picture of zealous activity, where barrels full and empty are shipped or received. It is interesting to note that two members of the Guinness family have been raised to peerage, by virtue of public spirt closely allied to "XX".

QUEENSTOWN, FROM THE HARBOR. – The general view of the handsome city of Queenstown presented above gives a good idea of how it strikes the traveller who first beholds the famous Irish seaport form the waters of its spacious harbour. The noble pile on the right of the picture is the Catholic cathedral which, when entirely finished, will be one of the grandest temples of worship in Christendom. Owing to the high formation of the ground on which Queenstown is built, the houses rise in terraces, with a back ground, at most points, of umbrageous trees and green slopes. It is admitted to be one of the healthiest municipalities in the world, and, notwithstanding the large sea-faring element – usually "wild" after long ocean voyages – one of the best ordered in Great Britain and Ireland. Indeed, one of the practical arguments in favour of Irish autonomy is that the Irish cities and towns, which possess local government, as they all do, are quite as well governed as English cities and towns, and are, besides, much freer from crime and disorder. IN many of the Irish counties and burghs, recently, the judges have presented "white gloves" toe the grand juries to indicate that there was no criminal business to come before them – something without parallel in England.

HORSE SHOW, BALL'S BRIDGE, DUBLIN. – The annual Horse Show held at Ball's Bridge, Dublin, is one of the greatest attractions of the Irish metropolis. It occurs in the summer season, when everything beautiful in Ireland is at its best and when even things not beautiful cease to be repellent. All Europe knows the value of the Irish horse. The racer, the hunter and the charger are all renowned in cavalier circles, and have been bestridden by Emperors, Kings, Princes, Marshals, Generals and other grandees, to no end.

The once beautiful Empress of Austria used to delight in clearing "double quick-set hedges" and stone walls six feet high and upwards on the back of her noble Irish mare. Dragoon officers and other experts, from all over the world, frequent the Dublin Horse Show every year, and buy there liberally, but chiefly "mounts" for the officers of "crack regiments," who love the high mettle of the "clean timbered," short-coupled Irish saddle horse, whose rival is our own Kentucky thoroughbred. The show is attended by the elite of Great Britain and Ireland, as well as by enterprising "foreigners," and the sketch fully shows the quality of the patrons of the equine exposition. The premises are owned by the Royal Dublin Society, and there is accommodation for about 2,000 animals. The society has, up to date, expended €325,000 on improvements at Ball's Bridge.

O'CONNELL BRIDGE, DUBLIN. – Since the enlargement of the Irish municipal franchise, under the Gladstone regime, many of the Irish cities have elected aldermen who represent the national feelings of the people. In consequence of this, many streets and public structures, in Dublin and elsewhere, which had formerly borne English names, have been virtually re-christened. Among the thoroughfares so renamed is Sackville Street, now O'Connell Street, with Westmoreland and D'Olier Streets. This bridge has been greatly improved within the last twenty years. It commands a superb view of the main artery of Dublin's commercial life. At its southern end rises Farrell's masterly statue of William Smith O'Brien, the Young Ireland leader and "rebel" of 1848; and at its northern line the fine monument to O'Connell, after the model of the famed sculptor J. H. Foley, who died before its completion.

Hogan's striking statue of the Catholic Liberator, said to be the best extant, is placed in the City Hall, formerly the Royal Exchange. This is the statue that called forth Thomas Davis matchless apostrophe, "chisel the likeness of our Chief."

WATER WORKS CITY OF CORK. – This sketch shows the hill above the River Lee, on and along which are situated the excellent water works' buildings of the City of Cork. If, in many respects, Ireland, chiefly because of political excitement and social disasters, is backward of other countries richly endowed by nature, she is wealth indeed, in her deep, clear and rapid rivers, her crystal lakes and her pellucid springs and streamlets. "The best watered country in Europe," was the verdict of Arthur Young, the eminent English traveller and writer, on Ireland in the last century. Cork, which has two fine streams, and numerous gushing springs, is particularly blessed in this regards, especially since her modern water works, in every way abreast of times, were constructed. The water supply is copious and the cost is reasonable. In the matter of municipal government, Ireland has proved herself, in all her great cities, fully equal in ability to richer and freer, Albion – thus practically disposing of the old time slander, invented and propagated for political effect, that Irishmen have not the governing faculty. In the cities of Ireland, they have certainly shown themselves not inferior in governmental capacity to any other race.

WEST PASSAGE, CO. CORK.

The place shown in the above sketch is situated on the west shore of the estuary of the river Lee, six miles from the City of Cork, and is a seaport town of some importance. It is generally called West Passage, to distinguish it from the other town of Passage, near the mouth of the river Suir in the County of Waterford. Of the late years West Passage has attained prominence as an agreeable watering place, and is more frequented by invalids in search of quite sea-bathing. Many foreign tourists also visit in the summer months. It is now recognized as an indispensable marine station and shipping point for Cork City. Ship building is one of the local industries. No boats of over 500 tons burden can pass up the river beyond Passage, and vessels of heavier tonnage are compelled to discharge their cargoes there for reshipment. Therefore, there is a lively business in "lighters" and this circumstance adds to the prosperity of the place. Carroll Mahone's ballad of the "Croppy Boy" had reference to Old Geneva Barracks and East Passage on the Suir –

"Upon yon river three tenders float;
The Priest's in one, if he isn't shot!
We hold this house for our Lord, the King
And Amen, say I, may all traitors swing!"

At Geneva Barracks that young man died,
And at Passage they have his body laid,
Good people, who live in peace and joy,
Breathe a prayer, drop a tear for the Croppy
Boy.

INISHANNON, COUNTY CORK. – The small but picturesque village of Innishannon – Gaelic Inis-Eoganain, Owenan's or Little Owen's Island – is situated on the left bank of the sparkling river Bandon, below here it receives the joint tribute of the Ballymahane and Brinny rivers, before it opens on the deep inlet of Kinsale Harbour, so famous in Irish history. It is only a few miles from the Old Head of Kinsale, and has in its neighbourhood many interesting ruins, including Ship-pool Castle, erected ages ago by the Anglo-Norman family of the Roches; and Dundaneere Castle, near the junction of the Bandon and Brinny rivers. Innishannon itself is a modest, quite Irish hamlet, neatly kept and well arbored, as may be observed in the sketch. IN the main street appears the inevitable Irish jaunting car, the driver of which appears to be "asking his way" of the ladies on the sidewalk. He is, probably driving some English tourist to see the ruins of the old castle referred to, and is not quite sure of his "bearins". Every person he meets, however, will be glad to set him right, without "a tip" or the hope of being tipped; for in Ireland, except in a few overdone districts, the people are still hospitable, "and stranger is a holy name."

FERMOY, COUNTY OF CORK. – The fine town of Fermoy, in the eastern portion of the County of Cork, stands chiefly on the right bank of the Munster Blackwater, nineteen miles north-east from Cork City. In the Gaelic tongue, according to Professor Joyce, it is called Feara-muighe-Feine, shortened, according to O'Hevin, to Feara-Mueghe – "the Men of the Plain," and anglicized to Fermoy." It's most conspicuous relic of the past is the Cistercian Abbey, founded in the twelfth century, and now a ruin. In this town Sir John Anderson first introduced mail coaches, about a hundred years ago. They proved a great success and "made his fortune." These coaches found popular rivals subsequently in "Biaconi's Cars," – which flourished in the palmy days of O'Connell, before the railroads made, practically, and end of coaches and "long cars". A fine mountain chain rises form the river bank on the south side of Fermoy, the highest peak being that of Knock-an- Sceach – "Whitethorn Hill". It has an elevation of nearly 1,400 feet. The town is handsomely built and well laid out. The solid stone bridge, shown in the picture has thirteen arches, and was built in 1689 – the year before the battle of the Boyne. It is still an excellent sate of preservation, having been, of course frequently repaired. Fermoy contains a Catholic episcopal residence, a Catholic College, two Convents and Christian Brothers and National Schools. The population is estimated 6,500. The military barracks accommodate an English garrison of 3,000 men, horse and foot.

HOTEL AT GLENGARRIFF, CO. CORK. – Where once stood one of the residences of the O'Sullivan Beare family, the ancient lords of Glengarriff and the surrounding country, now stands the comfortable, modern hotel, pictured in this sketch. It is situated in a cosy, sheltered nook of Glengarriff Bay, and commands a fine view of the matchless scenery of the splendid region, whose manifold beauties have been depicted elsewhere. It must have been heartbreak to the gallant and chivalrous Donal O'Sullivan Beare, when, having done all the man could do in defence of the independence in his country, abandoned by the Spanish allies and deserted by kindred chiefs, who bent before the iron sway of the able and remorseless Elizabeth, he and his followers finally bade farewell to Glengarriff and sought asylum in the distant, and soon to be subjugated, fortresses of Breffni. Thomas Davis sang of the exodus plaintively thus:

I wandered at eve by Glengarriff's sweet water,
Half in the shade of the half in the moon,
And I thought of the time when the
Sacsonach
slaughter
Reddened the night and darkened the noon.

Mo nuar! Mon nuar! Mo nuar! I said –
When I think in this valley and sky,
Where true lovers and poets should sigh,
Of the time when its chieftain, O'Sullivan,
fled.

NEW BLARNEY CASTLE, CO. CORK. – The residence of Sir George Colthurst, situated in the old demesne which includes the famous ruins, is generally called New Blarney Castle. Although destitute of great age and romantic tradition, it is a splendid, lordly mansion, surrounded by luxuriant woods and convenient to the sparkling lake, out of whose waters, at stated periods, according to traditions of the poetical and imaginative peasantry, a heard of enchanted white cows emerge to graze upon the verdant banks. Another tradition connected with the lake is to the effect that the Earl of Clancarty, who owned the estate at the time of the Revolution, and who forfeited it through supporting the cause of the Stuarts, threw all of his plate and other riches into the water, so that it might not fall into the hands of the enemy. It is said that three of the McCarthy's hold the secret of the exact spot where the treasure is deposited, and when any of the number is dying he communicates the secret to another member of the family. The secret is not be revealed until a McCarthy is once more the owner of Blarney. The Colthursts, however, do not appear to be much disturbed by the legend and enjoy themselves greatly in their fine residence, of which the sketch gives a comprehensive view.

FRONT VIEW, ST. MARY'S CHURCH, CORK. – We give in this sketch a view of St. Mary's Dominican Church, from the river front. Built after the Grecian model, with a graceful portico of six Ionic columns, it presents but little of the aspect of the average Catholic or Protestant church in Ireland. The apex of the pediment is surrounded by a statue of the Virgin, heroic in proportions, and the head coroneted by an aureole of exquisite design and finish. Behind St. Mary's rise the towers of other edifices, devoted to religious purposes, and the summit of the famous steeple of St. Anne's of Shandon is seen in the background. Cork City justly boasts of some of the most beautiful, as well as historic, churches in Ireland, among them St. Finn- Barr's Cathedral, with which we have dealt in another sketch. St. Mary's is comparatively modern, but always attracts a great amount of attention from travellers and visitors because of the unique character of the architecture. The Dominican clergy, to whose use it is assigned, are noted for their fervid eloquence and, in consequence, the masses at this beautiful temple of worship are always largely attended. Interiorly the church is finished in a manner that perfectly harmonizes with the elegance of its exterior. The criticism is frequent, however, that were it not for the statue of the Virgin above the pediment, St. Mary's might easily be mistaken for a structure devoted to secular purposes.

MACROOM CASTLE, CO. CORK. – These imposing, ivy-garlanded ruins stand close to the town which gives them name, on appoint of land formed by the confluence of the Lee and Sullane rivers. Here the latter stream is merged in the longer river and their united waters flow on in stately volume to the sea. The name Macroom is derived from the Gaelic Maigh –Cruim, which according to Professor Addey, signifies "Plain of Crom, who was the Jupiter Tonans of the Irish; and here the second order of Druids, the Bards, held their meetings, even after the introduction of Christianity". It is said that the castle, which dates from the time of Kind John, was originally founded by the O'Flynn family, from whom it derived its ancient Gaelic name of Caslean-i-Fhlionn, or O'Flynn's castle. During the old wars it was often taken and retaken. In 1649, Lord Broghill, Cromwell's general, hanged Bishop MacEagan, of Ross, for refusing to ask the Irish garrison to surrender. Instead, according to Dr. Madden's poem he warned his compatriots thus;-

"Remember, tis writ in our annals of blood,
Our countrymen never relied on the faith
Of truce, or of treaty, but reason ensued –
And the issue of every delusion wad death!"
He died on the scaffold, in front of those walls
Where the blackness of ruin is seen from afar;
And the gloom of its desolate aspect recalls
The blackest of Broghill's achievements in war!

GRATTAN BRIDGE, DUBLIN. – Since the extension of the Irish voting power, under the Gladstone regime, the chief municipalities of Ireland, by their Aldermen, or Councillors, have asserted the national sentiment by substituting Irish for English names of streets and structures, wherever opportunity offers. Henry Grattan, the most gifted of Irish orators, and the founder of the " Constitution of 1782", which gave Ireland parliamentary independence for eighteen years, has given name to the bridge shown in the picture, which formerly bore the title of Essex Bridge. The latter was first constructed in 1996, while Arthur, Earl of Essex, was viceroy, but a new bridge, modelled on that of Westminster, was built in 1756 and remained in position until 1874, when the existing structure was put up by the Dublin Port and Docks Board.

It connects Capel and Parliament streets – respectively on the north and south banks of the river Liffey, which almost divides Dublin in two. It is the direct route to the Royal Exchange and Dublin Castle – the seat of English government in Ireland. The bridge is fifty feet in width at the driveway and pathways for pedestrians, twelve feet wide, on each side, make it sufficiently capacious for traffic and travel. The Corporation of Dublin named it Grattan.

ALONG THE QUAYS, DUBLIN. – No Dubliner will fail to recognize the above sketch of the noble Quays along the lower course of the river Liffey, with distant views of the "Metal" and O'Connell bridges, and the splendid dome of the Custom House towering proudly above the adjoining structures. Usually a lone of white letters, follows the arch of the Metal Bridge and is an advertisement, a la R.J. Gunning & Co., of Halloway's Pills and Ointment, which have done duty for all Irish ailments beyond "the memory of the oldest inhabitant". The "ads" of the time-honoured firm can, it is said, be found in the caves of the Antrim coast and on the peak of Mangerton, just as those of "Mrs. Winslow's Soothing Syrup" are to be found in the caverns of the Garden of Gods and on the summit of Pike's Peak. But our artist has omitted the "ad." Down by O'Connell Bridge, on Aston Quay, may be observed the western gable of the old Hibernian House, controlled by McBirney & Co. – formerly McBirney, Collins & Co. – a Marshall Field wholesale establishment of the Irish capital. The dear, familiar old Quays of Dublin! In looking upon them, the true Irishman feels himself borne back on the wings of love to the fair, but widowed, city, which of old possessed a national senate house – at once the cradle of genius and the tomb of liberty! Freedom, in Ireland, smiles at the name of Grattan and frowns at that of Castlereagh. Burgh Quay, on which stood O'Connell's "Conciliation Hall, " lies on the right bank of the Liffey, just beyond O'Connell Bridge.

THE SQUARE, FERMOY, CO. CORK. – As Fermoy is a garrison town, its public square is frequently the scene of military parades and manoeuvres, especially in the summer season, when "the bold solider boys," in flaming scarlet, can show off their marital figures to advantage before adoring cooks and nurse maids. The town is one of the best built in size in Ireland, and has the advantage of standing on the storied banks of the lovely Munster Blackwater, whose name is synonym of sylvan beauty. Notwithstanding its present aspect of comparative importance and prosperity, Fermoy was a somewhat insignificant place until about the first quarter of this century. In the vicinity are the ruins of the venerable Abbey of Bridgetown – the shrine and burial place of the once powerful and warlike Norman-Irish family of the Roches. Castletown Roche – formerly the homestead patrimony of the family – is in the neighbourhood
of the Abbey. The Roches, who had dispossessed the Milesian Irish in the days of Henry II, were themselves dispossessed by the Cromwellians, and Charles II., when restored to the throne, with characteristic ingratitude, for they had lost everything in his father's cause, refused to reinstate them. The last know representative of the direct line of this family died in poverty or holding menial positions.

CITY OF CORK – The sketch gives a general view of the world-famed City of Cork, taken from one of the surrounding vantage points. Modern enterprise and progress have swept away many of the old landmarks. Narrow streets and dingy lanes have been widened and otherwise improved, but many are still contracted and gloomy, and present a very decided contrast to the fine thoroughfares at the traverse of the better portion of the city built on "the island", formed by two branches of the river Lee. We have dealt in another sketch with the Mardyke, running parallel to the road, nearly two miles in extent and beautifully shaded by lofty elms, which interlace their umbrageous boughs, and form, in summer, a most agreeable arbor. The Queen's College, the Cathedral of St. Finn Barr and the Church of St. Anne of Shandon are objects of interest to the traveller. Of the latter, Rev. Francis Mahoney, "Father Pront", wrote the celebrated ballad, a quotation from which will be given in a more elaborate sketch of the church.

Of the time when its chieftain, O'Sullivan, fled.

NEW BLARNEY CASTLE, CO. CORK. – This castle, if neither the finest nor the most ancient, is, nevertheless, the most celebrated of ruined Irish fortresses, because of the alleged miraculously persuasive qualities of its worldrenowned "stone", which "whoever kisses, never misses to grow eloquent". About all that now remains of the once extensive castle, which was built by Cormac McCarthy, Lord of Muskerry, in the middle of the fifteenth century is the "donjon Keep", which rises to an altitude of one hundred and twenty feet, is of square configuration and has walls of great thickness. In ancient times, before the era of villainous saltpetre and cannon balls, it must have been a hopeless place on which to attempt an assault. Although there has been somewhat serious controversy relative to the identity of the "true Blarney stone", it is now generally conceded that it forms part of the face of the tower wall, several feet below the parapet, and bears the date of erection, A.D. 1446 and an almost illegible inscription in Latin. It is now secured in the wall by an iron clamp, as it was knocked out of place by a cannon ball during "Lord Broghill's siege of the castle in 1643. None but the agile and reckless can kiss the "true Blarney Stone". All others satisfy themselves with a substitute placed so conveniently that the osculator's neck is not imperilled.

ST. VINCENT'S CHURCH, SUNDAY'S WELL, CORK.- The Sketch shows, seated picturesquely on an eminence above the river Lee, the Catholic Church of St. Vincent, which is the principal ecclesiastical edifice in the suburb of the city of Cork, known as Sunday's Well. It is also called from an ancient spring, said to have been sacred to Druid rites before the era of Christianity in Ireland, and afterward utilized by the Catholic Fathers for baptismal purposes. The spring contains water peculiarly clear and cold, absolutely devoid of mineral flavour and much prized by the inhabitants of the district. Owing to its fine situation, Sunday's Well was, formerly, much visited by the citizens of Cork, and many handsome homes existed there. The changes wrought by time however, have not been favourable to the district as a fashionable residence locality, and the well-to-do people now build their dwellings elsewhere. Yet Sunday's Well is by no means abandoned, and the view to be obtained from the hill above the Lee, is regarded as one of the finest in the beauteous South of Ireland. There is a tradition to the effect that the gallant and ill-fated Lord Edward Fitzgerald resided, "on his keeping", in the vicinity, during the month of April, 1798. On his return to Dublin, he was captured, severely wounded and died in prison.

ST. MARY'S CHURCH, CORK. - The sketch displays a wide sweep of the river Lee as it dashes on to St. Patrick's Bridge, shown in the distance, with masts of shipping forming a forest above its battlements, and a fleet of small boats moored in the rapid stream. On the left rises the graceful portico of the Dominican Church of St. Mary's which is Hellenic in almost every point of its graceful architecture. The hexastyle portico of the Ionic order, is the admiration of all visitors to the City of Cork. The figure of the patron saint in marble, rises about the pediment, and can be seen at a great distance up and down the river Lee. Interiorly, the sacred edifice also recalls the nameless grace that characterizes everything arranged after the Grecian model. Of all the Orders of the Catholic Church, the Dominican is most noted for the beauty and finish of its architectural designs. To this great Order belonged the celebrated preacher and lecturer, the Rev. Thomas Burke, generally called "Father Tom" – an orator who had much of the power that O'Connell possessed of charming the impressionable Irish people. His eloquent voice was heard often in St. Mary's Church, and the Irish people felt the bereavement to be personnel to each one, when the premature death of the brilliant conqueror of the sensational English "historian", Froude, was announced only a few years ago.

Custom House

THE HISTORY OF DUBLIN

The City of Dublin can trace its origin back more than 1,000 years, and for much of this time it has been Ireland's principal city and the cultural, educational and industrial centre of the island.

Founding and Early History

The earliest reference to Dublin is sometimes said to be found in the writings of Claudius Ptolemaeus (Ptolemy), the Egyptian-Greek astronomer and cartographer, around the year 140, who refers to a settlement called Eblana. This would seem to give Dublin a just claim to nearly two thousand years of antiquity, as the settlement must have existed a considerable time before Ptolemy became aware of it. Recently, however, doubt has been cast on the identification of Eblana with Dublin, and the similarity of the two names is now thought to be coincidental.

It is now thought that the Viking settlement was preceded by a Christian ecclesiastical settlement known as Duiblinn, from which Dyflin took its name. Beginning in the 9th and 10th century, there were two settlements where the modern city stands. The Viking settlement of about 841 was known as Dyflin, from the Irish Duiblinn (or "Black Pool", referring to a dark tidal pool where the River Poddle entered the Liffey on the site of the Castle Gardens at the rear of Dublin Castle), and a Gaelic settlement, Áth Cliath ("ford of hurdles") was further upriver, at the present day Father Mathew Bridge at the bottom of Church Street.[1] The Celtic settlement's name is still used as the Irish name of the modern city, though the first written evidence of it is found in the Annals of Ulster of 1368.[2] The modern English name came from the Viking settlement of Dyflin, which derived its name from the Irish Duiblinn. The Vikings, or Ostmen as they called themselves, ruled Dublin for almost three centuries, although they were expelled in 902 only to return in 917 and notwithstanding their defeat by the Irish High King Brian Boru at the Battle of Clontarf in 1014. From that date, the Norse were a minor political force in Ireland, firmly opting for a commercial life.[3] Viking rule of Dublin would end completely in 1171 when the city was captured by King Dermot MacMurrough of Leinster, with the aid of Anglo-Norman mercenaries. An attempt was made by the last Norse King of Dublin, Ascall mac Ragnaill, to recapture the city with an army he raised among his relations in the Scottish Highlands, where he was forced to flee after the city was taken, but the attempted reconquest failed and Ascall was killed.

The *Thingmote* was a raised mound, 40-foot (12 m) high and 240-foot (73 m) in circumference, where the Norsemen assembled and made their laws. It stood on the south of the river, adjacent to Dublin Castle, until 1685.[4] Viking Dublin had a large slave market. Thralls were captured and sold, not only by the Norse but also by warring Irish chiefs.

Dublin celebrated its millennium in 1988 with the slogan Dublin's great in '88'. The city is far older than that, but in that year, the Norse King Glun Iarainn recognised Máel Sechnaill II (Máel Sechnaill Mór), High King of Ireland, and agreed to pay taxes and accept Brehon Law. That date was celebrated, but might not be accurate: in 989 (not 988), Mael Seachlainn laid siege to the city for 20 days and captured it. This was not his first attack on the city. Dublin became the centre of English power in Ireland after the Norman invasion of the southern half of Ireland (Munster and Leinster) in 1169-71, replacing Tara in Meath — seat of the Gaelic High Kings of Ireland — as the focal point of Ireland's polity. On 15 May 1192 Dublin's first written Charter of Liberties was granted by John, Lord of Ireland, and was addressed to all his "French, English, Irish and Welsh subjects and friends". On 15 June 1229 his son Henry granted the citizens the right to elect a Mayor who was to be assisted by two provosts. By 1400, however, many of the Anglo-Norman conquerors were absorbed into the Gaelic culture, adopting the Irish language and customs, leaving only a small area of Leinster around Dublin, known as the Pale, under direct English control.

Late Medieval Dublin

After the Anglo-Normans taking of Dublin in 1171, many of the city's Norse inhabitants left the old city, which was on the south side of the river Liffey and built their own settlement on the north side, known as Ostmantown or "Oxmantown". Dublin became the capital of the English Lordship of Ireland from 1171 onwards and was peopled extensively with settlers from England and Wales. The rural area around the city, as far north as Drogheda, also saw extensive English settlement. In the 14th century, this area was fortified against the increasingly assertive Native Irish – becoming known as The Pale. In Dublin itself, English rule was centred on Dublin Castle. The city was also the main seat of the Parliament of Ireland from 1297, which was composed of landowners and merchants. Important buildings that date from this time include St Patrick's Cathedral, Christchurch Cathedral and St. Audoen's Church, all of which are within a kilometre of each other.

The inhabitants of the Pale developed an identity familiar from other settler-colonists of a beleaguered enclave of civilization surrounded by "barbarous natives". The siege mentality of medieval Dubliners is best illustrated by their annual pilgrimage to the area called Fiodh Chuilinn, or Holly Wood (rendered in English as Cullenswood) in Ranelagh, where, in 1209, five hundred recent settlers from Bristol had been massacred by the O'Toole clan during an outing outside the city limits. Every year on "Black Monday", the Dublin citizens would march out of the city to the spot where the atrocity had happened and raise a black banner in the direction of the mountains to challenge the Irish to battle in a gesture of symbolic defiance. This was still so dangerous that, until the 17th century, the participants had to be guarded by the city militia and a stockade against "the mountain enemy".

Medieval Dublin was a tightly knit place of around 5,000 to 10,000 people, intimate enough for every newly married citizen to be escorted by the mayor to the city bullring to kiss the enclosure for good luck. It was also very small in area, an enclave hugging the south side of the Liffey of no more than three square kilometres. Outside the city walls were suburbs such as the Liberties, on the lands of the Archbishop of Dublin, and Irishtown, where Gaelic Irish were supposed to live, having been expelled from the city proper by a 15th-century law.

Although the native Irish were not supposed to live in the city and its environs, many did so and by the 16th century, English accounts complain that Irish Gaelic was starting to rival English as the everyday language of the Pale.

Life in Medieval Dublin was very precarious. In 1348, the city was hit by the Black Death – a lethal bubonic plague that ravaged Europe in the mid-14th century. In Dublin, victims of the disease were buried in mass graves in an area still known as "Blackpitts". Though Archaeological excavations in the past ten years have found evidence of a tanning industry in this area, so the name "Blackpitts" may refer to the tanning pits which stained the surrounding area a deep dark colour. The plague recurred regularly in city until its last major outbreak in 1649.

Throughout the Middle Ages, the city paid tribute, protection money or "black rent" to the neighbouring Irish clans to avoid their predatory raids. In 1315, a Scottish army under Edward the Bruce burned the city's suburbs. As English interest in maintaining their Irish colony waned, the defence of Dublin from the surrounding Irish was left to the Fitzgerald Earls of Kildare, who dominated Irish politics until the 16th century. However, this dynasty often pursued their own agenda. In 1487, during the English Wars of the Roses, the Fitzgeralds occupied the city with the aid of troops from Burgundy and proclaimed the Yorkist Lambert Simnel to be King of England. In 1537, the same dynasty, led by Silken Thomas, who was angry at the imprisonment of Garret Fitzgerald, Earl of Kildare, besieged Dublin Castle. Henry VIII sent a large army to destroy the Fitzgeralds and replace them with English administrators.

This was the beginning of a much closer, though not always happy, relationship between Dublin and the English Crown.

16th and 17th Centuries

Dublin and its inhabitants were transformed by the upheavals of the 16th and 17th centuries in Ireland. These saw the first thorough English conquest of the whole island under the Tudor dynasty. While the Old English community of Dublin and the Pale were happy with the conquest and disarmament of the native Irish, they were deeply alienated by the Protestant reformation that had taken place in England, being almost all Roman Catholics. In addition, they were angered by being forced to pay for the English garrisons of the country through an extra-parliamentary tax known as "cess". Several Dubliners were executed for taking part in the Second Desmond Rebellion in the 1580s. The Mayoress of Dublin, Margaret Ball died in captivity in Dublin Castle for her Catholic sympathies in 1584 and a Catholic Archbishop, Dermot O'Hurley was hanged outside the city walls in the same year.

In 1592, Elizabeth I opened Trinity College Dublin (located at that time outside the city on its eastern side) as a Protestant University for the Irish gentry. However, the important Dublin families spurned it and sent their sons instead to Catholic Universities on continental Europe.

The Dublin community's discontent was deepened by the events of the Nine Years War of the 1590s, when English soldiers were required by decree to be housed by the townsmen of Dublin and they spread disease and forced up the price of food. The wounded lay in stalls in the streets, in the absence of a proper hospital. To compound disaffection in the city, in 1597, the English Army's gunpowder store in Wine tavern Street exploded accidentally, killing nearly 200 Dubliners. It should be noted, however, that the Pale community, however dissatisfied they were with English government, remained hostile to the Gaelic Irish led by Hugh O'Neill.

As a result of these tensions, the English authorities came to see Dubliners as unreliable and encouraged the settlement there of Protestants from England. These "New English" became the basis of the English administration in Ireland until the 19th century.

Protestants became a majority in Dublin in the 1640s, when thousands of them fled there to escape the Irish Rebellion of 1641. When the city was subsequently threatened by Irish Catholic forces, the Catholic Dubliners were expelled from the city by its English garrison. In the 1640s, the city was besieged twice during the Irish Confederate Wars, in 1646 and 1649.

However, on both occasions the attackers were driven off before a lengthy siege could develop.

In 1649, on the second of these occasions, a mixed force of Irish Confederates and English Royalists were routed by Dublin's English Parliamentarian garrison in the battle of Rathmines, fought on the city's southern outskirts.

In the 1650s after the Cromwellian conquest of Ireland, Catholics were banned from dwelling within the city limits under the vengeful Cromwellian settlement but this law was not strictly enforced. Ultimately, this religious discrimination led to the Old English community abandoning their English roots and coming to see themselves as part of the native Irish community.

By the end of the seventeenth century, Dublin was the capital of the English run Kingdom of Ireland – ruled by the Protestant New English minority. Dublin (along with parts of Ulster) was the only part of Ireland in 1700 where Protestants were a majority. In the next century it became larger, more peaceful and prosperous than at any time in its previous history.

From a Medieval to a Georgian City

By the beginning of the 18th century the English had established control and imposed the harsh Penal Laws on the Catholic majority of Ireland's population. In Dublin however the Protestant Ascendancy was thriving, and the city expanded rapidly from the 17th century onward. By 1700, the population had surpassed 60,000, making it the second largest city, after London, in the British Empire. Under the Restoration, Ormonde, the then Lord Deputy of Ireland made the first step toward modernising Dublin by ordering that the houses along the river Liffey had to face the river and have high quality frontages. This was in contrast to the earlier period, when Dublin faced away from the river, often using it as a rubbish dump.

During the 18th century, that many of the city's notable Georgian buildings and street scape schemes were built. Dublin started the 18th century as, in terms of street layout, a medieval city akin to Paris. In the course of the eighteenth century (as Paris would in the nineteenth century) it underwent a major rebuilding, with the Wide Streets Commission demolishing many of the narrow medieval streets and replacing them with large Georgian streets. Among the famous streets to appear following this redesign were Sackville Street (now called O'Connell Street), Dame Street, Westmoreland Street and D'Olier Street, all built following the demolition of narrow medieval streets and their amalgamation. Five major Georgian squares were also laid out; Rutland Square (now called Parnell Square) and Mountjoy Square on the northside, and Merrion Square, Fitzwilliam Square and Saint Stephen's Green, all on the south of the River Liffey. Though initially the most prosperous residences of peers were located on the northside, in places like Henrietta Street and Rutland Square, the decision of the Earl of Kildare (Ireland's premier peer, later made Duke of Leinster), to build his new townhouse, Kildare House (later renamed Leinster House after he was made Duke of Leinster) on the southside, led to a rush from peers to build new houses on the southside, in or around the three major southern squares.

In 1745 Jonathan Swift, then Dean of St.Patrick's, bequeathed his entire estate to found a hospital for "fools and mad" and on August 8, 1746, a Royal Charter was granted to St. Patrick's Hospital by George II. Crucially, following his experiences as a governor of the Bedlam hospital in London, Swift intended the hospital to be designed around the needs of the patient and left strict instructions on how patients were to be treated. The first psychiatric hospital to be built in Ireland, it is one of the oldest in the world and still flourishes today as one of the largest and most comprehensive in the country.

For all its Enlightenment sophistication in fields such as architecture and music (Handel's "Messiah" was first performed there in Fishamble street), 18th century Dublin remained decidedly rough around the edges. Its slum population rapidly increased fed by the mounting rural migration to the city and housed mostly in the north and south-west quarters of the city. Rival gangs known as the "Liberty Boys", mostly Protestant weavers from the Liberties and the "Ormonde Boys", Catholic butchers from Ormonde Market on the northside, fought bloody street battles with each other,[10] sometimes heavily armed and with numerous fatalities. It was also common for the Dublin crowds to hold violent demonstrations outside the Irish Parliament when the members passed unpopular laws.

One of the effects of continued rural migration to Dublin was that its demographic balance was again altered, Catholics becoming the majority in the city again in the late 18th century.

Rebellion, Union and Catholic Emancipation

Until 1800 the city housed the Parliament of Ireland. While parliament was independent, both houses were the exclusive preserve of planters or Old English aristocracy. By the late 18th century, the Ascendancy class of Irish Protestants - who were mostly descendants of British settlers - came to regard Ireland as their native country. This 'Patriot Parliament' successfully agitated at Westminster for increased autonomy and better terms of trade with Great Britain and the Colonies. From 1778 the Penal Law, which discriminated against Roman Catholics in many areas of life, were gradually repealed, pushed along by liberals such as Henry Grattan. (See Ireland 1691-1801) However, under the influence of the American and French revolutions, some Irish radicals went a step further and formed the United Irishmen to create an independent, non-sectarian and democratic republic. United Irish leaders in Dublin included Napper Tandy, Oliver Bond and Edward Fitzgerald. Wolfe Tone, the leader of the movement, was also from Dublin.

The United Irishmen planned to take Dublin in a street rising in 1798, but their leaders were arrested and the city occupied by a large British military presence shortly before the rebels could assemble. There was some local fighting in the city's outskirts - such as Rathfarnham, but the city itself remained firmly under control during the 1798 rebellion.

The Protestant Ascendancy was shocked by the events of the 1790s, as was the British government. In response to them, in 1801 under the Irish Act of Union, which merged the Kingdom of Ireland with the Kingdom of Great Britain to form the United Kingdom of Great Britain and Ireland the Irish Parliament voted itself out of existence and Dublin lost its political status as a capital.

Though the city's growth continued, it suffered financially from the loss of parliament and more directly from the loss of the income that would come with the arrival of hundreds of peers and MPs and thousands of servants to the capital for sessions of parliament and the social season of the viceregal court in Dublin Castle. Within a short few years, many of the finest mansions, including Leinster House, Powerscourt House and Aldborough House, once owned by peers who spent much of their year in the capital, were for sale. Many of the city's once elegant Georgian neighbourhoods rapidly became slums. In 1803, Robert Emmet, the brother of one of the United Irish leaders launched another one-day rebellion in the city, however, it was put down easily and Emmet himself was hanged, drawn and quartered.

In 1829 the wealthier Irish Catholics recovered full citizenship of the United Kingdom. This was partly as a result of agitation by Daniel O'Connell, who organised mass rallies for Catholic Emancipation in Dublin among other places.

In 1840, Thomas Drummond, the Liberal Under-Secretary for Ireland, passed the Corporation Act, which totally reformed local government in Ireland. In Dublin this meant that the old franchise system, based on Protestant property holders and guild members was abolished and the vote for Dublin Corporation was granted to all property holders of over ten pounds per year.

This meant that Catholics, having been excluded from municipal government since the 1690s, became a 2-1 majority in the electorate. Daniel O'Connell, as a result, was elected Mayor in 1841, the first elections held with the new franchise.

O'Connell also campaigned unsuccessfully for a restoration of Irish legislative autonomy or Repeal of the Union. He organised mass rallies known as "Monster Meetings" in order to pressure the British government to concede the return of the Irish Parliament, abolished in 1801 under the Act of Union, to Dublin. The climax of his campaign was supposed to be a rally at Clontarf, just north of the city, which was chosen for its symbolic importance due to the Battle of Clontarf in 1014. Hundreds of thousands of people were expected to attend the meeting, but the British government banned in and sent in troops to suppress it. O'Connell backed down and his movement split and lost momentum.

O'Connell is also remembered among trade unionists in the city to this day for calling on the British army to suppress a strike during his tenure.

Late 19th Century

After Emancipation and with the gradual extension of the right to vote in British politics, Irish nationalists (mainly Catholics) gained control of Dublin's municipal government with the reform of local government in 1840, Daniel O'Connell being the first Catholic Mayor in 150 years. Increasing wealth prompted many of Dublin's Protestant and Unionist middle classes to move out of the city proper to new suburbs such as Ballsbridge, Rathmines and Rathgar - which are still distinguished by their graceful Victorian architecture. A new railway also connected Dublin with the middle class suburb of Dún Laoghaire, renamed Kingstown in 1821.

Dublin, unlike Belfast in the north, did not experience the full effect of the industrial revolution and as a result, the number of unskilled unemployed was always high in the city.

Industries like the Guinness brewery, Jameson Distillery, and Jacob's biscuit factory provided the most stable employment. New working class suburbs grew up in Kilmainham and Inchicore around them. Another major employer was the Dublin Tramways system, run by a private company - the Dublin United Tramway Company. By 1900 Belfast had a larger population than Dublin, though it is smaller today.

In 1867, the Irish Republican Brotherhood or 'Fenians', attempted an insurrection aimed at the ending of British rule in Ireland. However, the rebellion was badly organised and failed to get off the ground. In Dublin, fighting was confined to the suburb of Tallaght. Several thousand Fenians (estimated at between 4-8,000 men) marched out to Tallaght Hill, and some fought a brief skirmish with the police at the Royal Irish Constabulary barracks in Tallaght. However, due to poor leadership and unclear plans, they dispersed shortly thereafter, several hundred were arrested. The failure of this rebellion did not mark the end of nationalist violence however.

An attempt to free three Fenian prisoners in Manchester killed a guard, for which three Fenians were hanged. Dublin saw mass demonstrations in solidarity with those executed and an Amnesty Campaign for the other Fenian prisoners.

In 1882, an offshoot of the Fenians, who called themselves the Irish National Invincibles, assassinated two prominent members of the British administration with surgical knives in the Phoenix Park, in reprisal for the introduction of Coercion Acts against the Land League and the RIC killing of two demonstrators in County Mayo. The incident became known as the Phoenix Park murders and was universally condemned.

Under the 1898 Local Government Act, the electorate to Dublin Corporation was expanded to include all rate payers. Greater powers of administration were also devolved to local government, as part of a political strategy by the Conservative party of "killing Home Rule with kindness", or placating Irish nationalist grievances.

Monto

Although Dublin declined in terms of wealth and importance after the Act of Union, it grew steadily in size throughout the 19th century. By 1900, the population was over 400,000. While the city grew, so did its level of poverty. Though described as "the second city of the (British) Empire", its large number of tenements became infamous, being mentioned by writers such as James Joyce. An area called *Monto* (in or around *Montgomery* Street off Sackville Street) became infamous also as the British Empire's biggest red light district, its financial viability aided by the number of British Army barracks and hence soldiers in the city, notably the *Royal Barracks* (later Collins Barracks and now one of the locations of Ireland's National Museum). *Monto* finally closed in the mid-1920s, following a campaign against prostitution by the Roman Catholic Legion of Mary, its financial viability having already been seriously undermined by the withdrawal of soldiers from the city following the Anglo-Irish Treaty (December 1921) and the establishment of the Irish Free State (6 December 1922).

The Lockout

In 1913, Dublin experienced one of the largest and most bitter labour disputes ever seen in Britain or Ireland - known as the Lockout. James Larkin, a militant syndicalist trade unionist, founded the Irish Transport and General Worker's Union (ITGWU) and tried to win improvements in wages and conditions for unskilled and semi-skilled workers. His means were negotiation and if necessary sympathetic strikes. In response, William Martin Murphy, who owned the Dublin Tram Company, organised a cartel of employers who agreed to sack any ITGWU members and to make other employees agree not to join it. Larkin in turn called the Tram workers out on strike, which was followed by the sacking, or "lockout", of any workers in Dublin who would not resign from the union. Within a month, 25,000 workers were either on strike or locked out. Demonstrations during the dispute were marked by vicious rioting with the Dublin Metropolitan Police, which left three people dead and hundreds more injured. James Connolly in response founded the Irish Citizen Army to defend strikers from the police. The lockout lasted for six months, after which most workers, many of whose families were starving, resigned from the union and returned to work.

The End of British Rule

In 1914, after nearly three decades of agitation, Ireland seemed on the brink of Home Rule (or self-government), however, instead of a peaceful handover from direct British rule to limited Irish autonomy, Ireland and Dublin saw nearly ten years of political violence and instability that eventually resulted in a much more complete break with Britain than Home Rule would have represented. By 1923, Dublin was the capital of the Irish Free State, an all but independent Irish state, governing 26 of Ireland's 32 counties.

Howth Gun Running 1914

Unionists, predominantly concentrated in Ulster, though also with significant numbers in Dublin and throughout the country, resisted the introduction of Home Rule and founded the Ulster Volunteers (UVF) - a private army - to this end. In response, nationalists founded their own army, the Irish Volunteers, to make sure Home Rule became a reality. In April 1914, thousands of German weapons were imported by the UVF into the north (see Larne gunrunning). Some within the Irish Volunteers, and other nationalists unconnected with that organisation, attempted to do the same in July. The crew of *Asgard* successfully landed a consignment of surplus German rifles and ammunition at Howth, near Dublin. Shortly after the cargo was landed, British troops from the Scottish Borderers regiment tried to seize them but were unsuccessful. The soldiers were jeered by Dublin crowds when they returned to the city centre and they retaliated by opening fire at Bachelors Walk, killing three people. Ireland appeared to be on the brink of civil war by the time the Home Rule Bill was actually passed in September 1914. However, the outbreak of World War I led to its shelving. John Redmond, the leader of the Volunteers and the Irish Parliamentary Party, called on nationalists to join the British Army. This caused a split in the Volunteers. Thousands of Irishmen did join (particularly those from working class areas, where unemployment was high) and many died in the war. The majority, who followed Redmond's leadership, formed the National Volunteers.

A militant minority kept the title of Irish Volunteers, some of whom were now prepared to fight against, rather than with British forces for Irish independence.

Easter Rising 1916

In April 1916 about 1,250 armed Irish republicans under Padraig Pearse staged what became known as the Easter Rising in Dublin in pursuit not of Home Rule but of an Irish Republic. One of the rebels' first acts was to declare this Republic to be in existence. The rebels were composed of Irish Volunteers and the much smaller Irish Citizen Army under James Connolly.

The rising saw rebel forces take over strongpoints in the city, including the Four Courts, Stephen's Green, Boland's mill, the South Dublin Union and Jacobs Biscuit Factory and establishing their headquarters at the General Post Office building in O'Connell street.

They held for a week until they were forced to surrender to British troops. The British deployed artillery to bombard the rebels into submission, sailing a gunboat named the Helga up the Liffey and stationing field guns at Cabra, Phibsborough and Prussia street. Much of the city centre was destroyed by shell fire and around 450 people, about half of them civilians, were killed, with another 1,500 injured. Fierce combat took place along the grand canal at Mount street, where British troops were repeatedly ambushed and suffered heavy casualties. In addition, the rebellion was marked by a wave of looting and lawlessness by Dublin's slum population and many of the city centre's shops were ransacked. The rebel commander, Patrick Pearse surrendered after a week, in order to avoid further civilian casualties. Initially, the rebellion was generally unpopular in Dublin, due to the amount of death and destruction it caused, the opinion by some that it was bad timing to irreverently hold it at Easter and also due to the fact that many Dubliners had relatives serving in the British Army.

Though the rebellion was relatively easily suppressed by the British military and initially faced with the hostility of most Irish people, public opinion swung gradually but decisively behind the rebels, after 16 of their leaders were executed by the British military in the aftermath of the Rising. In December 1918 the party now taken over by the rebels, Sinn Féin, won an overwhelming majority of Irish parliamentary seats. Instead of taking their seats in the British House of Commons, they assembled in the Lord Mayor of Dublin's residence and proclaimed the Irish Republic to be in existence and themselves Dáil Éireann (the Assembly of Ireland) - its parliament.

War of Independence 1919-21

Between 1919 and 1921 Ireland experienced the Irish War of Independence -a guerrilla conflict between the British forces and the Irish Volunteers, now reconstituted as the Irish Republican Army. The Dublin IRA units waged an urban guerrilla campaign against police and the British army in the city. In 1919, the violence began with small numbers of IRA men (known as "the Squad") under Michael Collins assassinating police detectives in the city. By late 1920, this had expanded into much more intensive operations, including regular gun and grenade attack on British troops. The IRA in Dublin tried to carry out three shooting or bombing attacks a day.

Such was the regularity of attacks on British patrols, that the Camden-Aungier streets area (running from the military barracks at Portobello to Dublin Castle) was nicknamed the "Dardanelles" (site of the Gallipoli campaign) by British soldiers.

The conflict produced many tragic incidents in the city, of which a number are still remembered today. In September 1920, 18-year-old IRA man Kevin Barry was captured during an ambush on Church street in the north city in which three British soldiers were killed. Barry was hanged for murder on November 1, despite a campaign for leniency because of his youth. Another celebrated republican martyr was IRA gunman Seán Treacy, who was killed in a shoot out on Talbot street in October 1920 after a prolonged manhunt for him. The British forces, in particular the Black and Tans, often retaliated to IRA actions with brutality of their own. One example of this was the Black and Tans burning of the town of Balbriggan, just north of Dublin in September 1920 and the "Drumcondra murders" of February 1921, when Auxiliary Division troops murdered two suspected IRA men in the city's northern suburb.

The bloodiest single day of these "troubles" (as they were known at the time) in Dublin was Bloody Sunday on November 21, 1920, when the Michael Collins' "Squad" assassinated 18 British agents (see Cairo gang) around the city in the early hours of the morning. The British forces retaliated by opening fire on a Gaelic football crowd in Croke Park in the afternoon, killing 14 civilians and wounding 65. In the evening, three republican activists were arrested and killed in Dublin Castle.

In response to the escalating violence, the British troops mounted a number of major operations in Dublin to try to locate IRA members. From January 15–17, 1921, they cordoned off an area of the north inner city bounded by Capel st, Church st and North King st, allowing no one in or out and searching house to house for weapons and suspects. In February they repeated the process in the Mountjoy Square and then the Kildare st/Nassau st areas. However, these curfews produced few results. The largest singe IRA operation in Dublin during the conflict came on May 25, 1921, the IRA Dublin Brigade burned down The Custom House, one of Dublin's finest buildings, which housed the headquarters of local government in Ireland.

However, the British were soon alerted and surrounded the building. Five IRA men were killed and over 80 captured in the operation, which was a publicity coup but a military disaster for the IRA.

Civil War 1922-23

Following a truce (declared on July 11, 1921), a negotiated peace known as the Anglo-Irish Treaty between Britain and Ireland was signed. It created a self-governing twenty-six county Irish state, known as the Irish Free State. However, it also disestablished the Irish Republic, which many in the nationalist movement and the IRA in particular felt they were bound by oath to uphold. This triggered the outbreak of the Irish Civil War of 1922-23, when the intransigent republicans took up arms against those who had accepted a compromise with the British. The Civil war began in Dublin, where Anti-Treaty forces under Rory O'Connor took over the Four Courts and several other buildings in April 1922, hoping to provoke the British into restarting the fighting. This put the Free State, led by Michael Collins and Arthur Griffith into the dilemma of facing British military re-occupation or fighting their own former comrades in the Four Courts.

After some prevarication and after Winston Churchill had actually ordered British troops to assault the rebels, Collins decided he had to act and borrowed British artillery to shell the republicans in the Four Courts. They surrendered after a two-day (28–30 June 1922) artillery bombardment by Free State troops but some of their IRA comrades occupied O'Connell Street, which saw street fighting for another week before the Free State army secured the capital. (See Battle of Dublin). Over 60 combatants were killed in the fighting, including senior republican Cathal Brugha. About 250 civilians are also thought to have been killed or injured, but the total has never been accurately counted. Oscar Traynor conducted some guerrilla operations south of the city until his capture in late July 1922. Ernie O'Malley, the republican commander for the province of Leinster was captured after a shootout in the Ballsbridge area in November 1922. On December 6, 1922, the IRA assassinated Sean Hales a member of Parliament as he was leaving Leinster House in Dublin city centre, in reprisal for the executions of their prisoners by the Free State. The following day, the four leaders of the republicans in the Four Courts (Rory O'Connor, Liam Mellows, Dick Barret and Joe McKelvey) were executed in revenge. Dublin was relatively quiet thereafter, although guerrilla war raged in the provinces. The new Free State government eventually suppressed this insurrection by mid-1923. In April, Frank Aiken, IRA chief of staff, ordered the anti-treaty forces to dump their arms and go home. The civil war left a permanent strain of bitterness in Irish politics that did much to sour the achievement of national independence.

Independence

Dublin had suffered severely in the period 1916-1922. It was the scene of a week's heavy street fighting in 1916 and again on the outbreak of the civil war in 1922. The casualties in Dublin of the revolutionary period from 1916-1923 come to about 1,000 dead - 482 killed in the 1916 Easter Rising, another 309 fatal casualties in the 1919-21 War of Independence and finally about 200 killed in the city in the Civil War of 1922-23.[19]

Many of Dublin's finest buildings were destroyed at this time; the historic General Post Office (GPO) was a bombed out shell after the 1916 Rising; James Gandon's Custom House was burned by the IRA in the War of Independence, while one of Gandon's surviving masterpieces, the Four Courts had been seized by republicans and bombarded by the pro-treaty army. (Republicans in response senselessly booby trapped the Irish Public Records Office, destroying one thousand years of archives). These buildings were later re-built.

The new state set itself up as best it could. Its Governor-General was installed in the former Viceregal Lodge, residence of the British Lord Lieutenant of Ireland, because it was thought to be one of the few places where he was not in danger from republican assassins. Parliament was set up temporarily in the Duke of Leinster's old palace, Leinster House, where it has remained ever since. Over time, the GPO, Custom House and Four Courts were rebuilt. While major schemes were proposed for Dublin, no major remodelling took place initially.

The "Emergency"

Ireland was officially neutral during the Second World War. So much so that it was not even called "the war" in Irish discourse, but "The Emergency". Although Dublin escaped the mass bombing of the war due to Ireland's neutrality, the German air-force bombed Dublin on May 31, 1941, and hit the North Strand – a working-class district in the north inner city – killing 34 Irish civilians and wounding another 90. The bombing was declared accidental, although many suspected that the bombing was deliberate revenge for de Valera's decision to send fire engines to aid the people of Belfast following major bombing in that city. One faction of the IRA hoped to take advantage of the war by getting German help and invading Northern Ireland. In December 1939 they successfully stole almost all the Irish Army's reserve ammunition in a raid on the Magazine Fort in Dublin's Phoenix Park. In retaliation, De Valera interned the IRA's members and executed several of them. The war years also saw rationing imposed on Dublin and the temporary enlargement of the small Jewish community by Jews who fled there from Nazi persecution.

Tackling the Tenements

The first efforts to tackle Dublin's extensive slum areas came on the foundation of the Iveagh Trust in 1891, and the Dublin Artisan Dwellings Company, but these could only help several thousand families. The main focus by government in 1900-1914 was in building 40,000 cottages for rural workers. Some public planning for the city was made in the first years of the Irish Free State and then effected after 1932, when Éamon de Valera came to power. With greater finances available, and lower wages due to the Great Depression, major changes began to take place. A scheme of replacing tenements with decent housing for Dublin's poor began.

Some new suburbs such as Marino and Crumlin were built but Dublin's inner city slums remained.

It was not until the 1960s that substantial progress was made in removing Dublin's tenements, with thousands of Dublin's working class population being moved to suburban housing estates around the edge of the city. The success of this project was mixed. Although the tenements were largely removed, such was the urgency of the providing new housing that little planning went into the building of the new public housing. New and growing suburbs like Tallaght, Coolock and Ballymun instantly acquired huge populations, of up to 50,000 people in Tallaght's case, without any provision of shops, public transport or employment. As a result, for several decades, these places became by-words for crime, drug abuse and unemployment. In recent years, such problems have eased somewhat, with the advent of Ireland's so-called 'Celtic Tiger' economic boom. Tallaght in particular has become far more socially mixed and now has very extensive commercial, transport and leisure facilities. Ballymun Flats, one of the State's few high-rise housing schemes, was largely demolished and re-designed in recent years.

Ironically however, given Ireland's new found economic prosperity, and consequent immigration, there is once again a housing shortage in the city. Increased employment has led to a rapid rise in the city's population. As a result, prices for bought and rented accommodation have risen sharply, leading to many younger Dubliners leaving the city to buy cheaper accommodation in counties Meath, Louth, Kildare and Wicklow, while still commuting daily to Dublin. This has arguably impacted negatively on the quality of life in the city - leading to severe traffic problems, long commuting times and urban sprawl.

Destruction of Georgian Dublin in 1960s

As part of the building programme that also cleared the inner city slums, from the 1950s onwards, historic Georgian Dublin came under concerted attack by the Irish Government's development policies. Whole swathes of 18th-century houses were demolished, notably in Fitzwilliam Street and St Stephen's Green, to make way for utilitarian office blocks and government departments. Much of this development was fuelled by property developers and speculators keen to cash in on the buoyant property markets of the 1960s, late 1970s and 1980s.

Many schemes were built by Government supporters with the intention of profitably letting to highly desirable State tenants such as government departments and State agencies. It has been proven that many buildings were approved by government ministers personally connected with the developers involved, often to the detriment of the taxpayer and the proper planning and preservation of Dublin city.

Some of this development was also encouraged by Ireland's dominant nationalist ideology of that era, which wanted to wipe away all physical reminders of Ireland's colonial past. An extreme example of this kind of thinking was the destruction of Nelson's Pillar in O'Connell Street in 1966. This statue of the famous British admiral was a Dublin landmark for a century, but was blown up by a small bomb shortly before the 50 year commemorations of the Easter Rising. In 2003, the Pillar was replaced as a landmark by the Dublin Spire which was erected on the same spot. A 120 m tall tapered metal pole, it is the tallest structure of Dublin city centre, visible for miles. It was assembled from seven pieces with the largest crane available in Ireland and is the tallest street sculpture in the world.

Far from the destructive practices of the 1960s diminishing as time went on, if anything they got steadily worse, with the concrete office blocks of earlier times being replaced with the idea of Georgian pastiche or replica offices in place of original 18th century stock. Whole swathes of Harcourt Street and St. Stephen's Green were demolished and rebuilt in such a fashion in the 1970s and 1980s, as were parts of Parnell Square, Kildare Street, North Great George's Street and many other areas around the city. Many saw this practice as an 'easy way out' for planners; a venerable Georgian front was maintained, whilst 'progress' was allowed to continue unhindered. This planning policy was pursued by Dublin Corporation until around 1990, when the forces of conservationism finally took hold.

However, it was not only sites associated with the British presence in Ireland that fell victim to Irish developers. Wood Quay where the oldest remains of Viking Dublin were located was also demolished, and replaced with the headquarters of Dublin's local government, though not without a long and acrimonious planning struggle between the government and preservationists. More recently there has been a similar controversy over plans to build the M50 motorway through the site of Carrickmines Castle, part of the Pale's southern frontier in medieval times. It has recently been alleged that much controversial building work in Dublin- —over green spaces as well as historic buildings—-was allowed as a result of bribery and patronage of politicians by developers. Since the late 1990s, there have been a series of tribunals set up to investigate corruption in Dublin's planning process.

Northern Troubles

Dublin was affected to varying degrees by "the Troubles" a civil conflict that raged in Northern Ireland from 1969 to the late 1990s. In 1972, angry crowds in Dublin burned down the British Embassy in Merrion Square in protest at the shooting of 13 civilians in Derry on Bloody Sunday (1972) by British troops.

However the city did not generally experience paramilitary violence directly, with the exception a period in the early to mid 1970s when it was the target of several loyalist bombings.

The 1972 and 1973 Dublin bombings killed 3 people and injured 185. The worst bomb attacks, however, occurred on Talbot street in 1974. The Dublin and Monaghan Bombings on May 17, 1974 were a series of terrorist attacks on Dublin and Monaghan in the Republic of Ireland which left 33 people dead (26 of them in Dublin), and almost 300 injured, the largest number of casualties in any single day in the Troubles. Although no organization claimed responsibility for the attacks at the time, loyalist paramilitaries from Northern Ireland (in particular the Ulster Volunteer Force) were widely blamed. In 1993 the Ulster Volunteer Force admitted they carried out the attacks. It has been widely speculated that the bombers were aided by members of the British security forces.

In the early 1970s the Irish government cancelled the hitherto annual Easter parade commemorating the Rising of 1916 and in 1976 banned it, fearing it was serving as a recruiting tool for illegal republican paramilitaries. Nevertheless, the Provisional republican movement organised a demonstration 10,000 strong on Easter Sunday. However the risks the Provisional IRA posed to the state were highlighted several months later when the organisation assassinated the British Ambassador to Ireland Christopher Ewart-Biggs near his home at Sandyford in south Dublin.

In 1981, there was considerable solidarity in Dublin with republican paramilitaries who were on hunger strike in Northern prisons. When Anti H-Block Irish republican protesters, over 15,000 strong, tried to storm the new British Embassy (reconstructed after the events of 1972) there took place several hours violent rioting with over 1,500 Gardaí, before the protesters were dispersed. Over 200 people were injured and dozens arrested.

Other, more peaceful demonstrations were held in the 1990s in Dublin, calling for the end of the Provisional IRA campaign in the North. The largest of these took place in 1993, when up to 20,000 people demonstrated in O'Connell Street after the IRA killed two children with a bomb in Warrington in northern England. Similar demonstrations occurred in 1995 and 1996 when the IRA ended its ceasefire, called in 1994, by bombing London and Manchester.

On 25 February 2006 rioting broke out between Gardaí and a group of hardline Irish Republicans protesting the march of a "Love Ulster", loyalist parade in O'Connell Street. The small group of political activists were joined by hundreds of local youths and running battles continued on O'Connell Street for almost three hours, where three shops were looted. The marchers themselves were bussed to Kildare street for a token march past Dáil Éireann which prompted some 200 or so rioters to move from O'Connell street to the Nassau street area, setting cars alight, attacking property, including the headquarters of the Progressive Democrats, before dispersing.

Regeneration of Dublin

Since the 1980s, there has been a greater awareness among Dublin's planners of the need to preserve Dublin's architectural heritage. Preservation orders have been put on most of Dublin's Georgian neighbourhoods. The new awareness was also reflected in the development of Temple Bar, the last surviving part of Dublin that contained its original medieval street plan.

In the 1970s, Córas Iompair Éireann (CIÉ), the state transport company, bought up many of the buildings in this area, with a view to building a large modern central bus station on the site with a shopping centre attached. However, most of the buildings had been rented by artists, producing a sudden and unexpected appearance of a 'cultural quarter' that earned comparisons with Paris's Left Bank. The vibrancy of the Temple Bar area led to demands for its preservation.

By the late 1980s, the bus station plans were abandoned and a master plan was put in place to maintain Temple Bar's position as Dublin's cultural heartland, with large-scale government support. That process has been a mixed success. While the medieval street plan has survived, rents have rocketed, forcing the artists elsewhere. They have been replaced by restaurants and bars which draw thousands of tourists but which has been criticised for over commercialisation and excessive alcohol consumption. Also, in the late 1980s the Grafton and Henry street areas were pedestrianised.

However, the real transformation of Dublin has occurred since the late 1990s, when the socalled 'Celtic Tiger' economic boom took effect. The city, previously full of derelict sites, has seen a building boom - especially the construction of new office blocks and apartments. The most visually spectacular of these developments is the International Financial Services Centre (IFSC)- a financial district almost a kilometre long situated along the North quays.

While the former tramways had been torn up in the 1950s in favour of buses, the new Luas tram service started in 2004. Though slow to develop, Dublin Airport had become the 16th busiest international airport by 2007.

Heroin Problem

In the late 1970s, '80s and '90s, Dublin suffered a serious wave of drug addiction and associated crime throughout its working-class areas. The introduction of the drug heroin into the inner city in the late 1970s accentuated social problems associated with unemployment, poor housing and poverty. These problems were twofold. Firstly, heroin addiction caused a wave of petty crime such as muggings, robbery and so forth as addicts tried to secure money for their next "fix". This made many of the affected areas all but un-inhabitable for the rest of the population. In addition, many addicts ultimately died from diseases such as AIDS and hepatitis caused by sharing needles. Secondly, the drug trade saw the establishment of serious organised crime syndicates in the city, whose use of violence led to many murders being committed. The most notorious of these killings was that of the journalist Veronica Guerin in 1996, who was killed by criminals she was investigating for a Sunday newspaper. The drugs problem led to a widespread anti-drugs movement, the most well known group was the Concerned Parents Against Drugs, which peaked in the mid-1990s, whose members tried to force drug dealers out of their neighbourhoods. The anti-drugs campaigners were accused of being vigilantes, or a front for Sinn Féin and the Provisional IRA, although this allegation has been vigorously disputed.

Although the problem of hard drugs in Dublin had been controlled somewhat, prior to the 2008 recession, through methadone programmes for addicts and better economic prospects for young people, it is by no means a thing of the past. As of 2011, heroin addiction and homelessness are huge problems across the inner city of Dublin.

Immigration

Dublin was traditionally a city of emigration, with high unemployment and a high birth rate forcing many of its inhabitants to leave Ireland for other countries, notably Britain and the United States. After 1700 a great number also arrived from the Irish countryside. However, the last fifteen years has seen this process reversed dramatically, with the Irish economic boom attracting immigrants from all over the world. The largest single group to arrive in the city has been returned Irish emigrants, but there has also been very large immigration from other nationalities. Dublin is now home to substantial communities of Chinese, Nigerians, Brazilians, Russians, Romanians and many others - especially from Africa and eastern Europe. After the accession of several eastern European countries into the European Union in 2004, eastern Europeans became the single largest immigrant group in Dublin. Poland was the most common single point of origin, with well over 150,000 young Poles having arrived in Ireland since late 2004; the majority are centered in Dublin and its environs.

Sara Bridge

(Island bridge) between extended South Circular Road and Conyngham Road. Named after Sarah Fane the wife of John Fane, tenth Earl of Westmoreland (Lord Lieutenant), who opened an iron frame hump-back bridge in 1794. Architect Alexander Stephens.

Seán Heuston Bridge (King's Bridge)

Seán Heuston Bridge (King's Bridge)

Named after Seán Heuston (1891 – 1916) Commandant in charge of the volunteers in the Mendicity Institute on Usher's Island. He was one of the sixteen leaders executed after the rising in 1916. Opened in 1828 and called King's Bridge (George IV), it no longer carries heavy traffic to the Lucan Road since the opening of the Frank Sherwin Bridge.

Grafton Street

Frank Sherwin Memorial Bridge

Frank Sherwin, a popular city councillor died Christmas 1981. It was agreed to
name the new bridge after him. The bridge was opened on 28 August 1982 below King's
Bridge (Sean Heuston) to take the increasing flow of traffic and afforded the facility of
Reversing the traffic flows on the North and South Quays. It was designed by Dublin
Corporation Road Section and build by Irishenco at a cost of £1.5 million.

St. Paul's Church

St Paul's dates from 1835-37, was designed by Patrick Byrne, and is one of the most prominent buildings on the city quays. Patrick Byrne was a prominent church architect of the time and was also responsible for St Audoen's on nearby High Street.

A fine portico with four Ionic columns fronts the church to the river in a very prominent site, especially for a catholic church which were usually sited on quieter back streets. The tower was completed in 1843 and gives the church a visibility along the quays except from the east where it is blocked by the dome of the Four Courts. It is currently closed to the public after a decline in numbers living in the parish.

The strong design has three large doors, of which the centre and largest leads to the church proper, which the other two leading to fine toplit stairwells which go to the balcony level. Recently railings have been added between the columns to prevent vandalism. The portico is topped by three statues.

Inside the main door is a large entrance hallway with a mosaic floor and a further internal wooden porch under the balcony. This leads to the main body of the church.

On entering the church, the height of the ceiling is obscured until you emerge out, around a third of the length of the church from the door, from under the organ balcony. Then your eye is drawn immediately to the altar and the large mural behind it.

Rory O'More Bridge

Named after one of the ring leaders of a plot to capture Dublin in October 1641. The participants were betrayed and O'More escaped by rowing up river to Island bridge. Opened in 1859 and called Queen Victoria Bridge it spans the site of Barrack Bridge, a wooden structure built in 1674 which was the second bridge to be built across the Liffey. This was found to interfere with the interests in a ferry which had previously plied in the same locality and a number of apprentices tried to destroy the new construction; twenty one of them were seized and committed to the Castle. When they were rescued, but four of them were killed in the fray and as a result of this the bridge was also known as Bloody Bridge.

James Larkin Statue, Clearys, O'Connell Street

James Joyce Bridge

It's a road bridge over the River Liffey, joining the South Quays TO Blackhall Place. Designed by the Spanish architect, artist and engineer Santiago Calatrava (born on July 28, 1951 in Valencia). The bridge was opened on June 16, 2003, it is named for the famous Dublin author James Joyce, whose short story "The Dead" is set in Number 15 Usher's Island, the house facing the bridge on the south side.

The Pro Cathedral, Marlborough Street

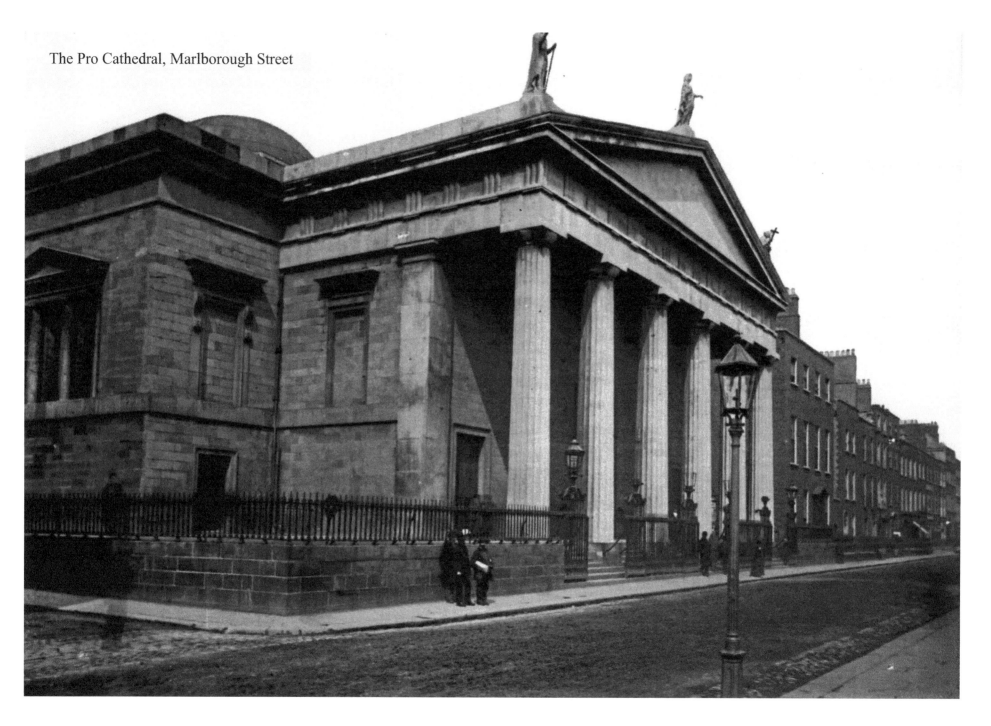

Mellor's Bridge (Queen Maeve Bridge)

Named after the Queen of Connaught who brought her whole army into
Ulster to seize a bull that was better looking than the one her husband had
in his possession. Built in 1764 and opened in 1768 this is the oldest bridge
spanning the river. Originally named Queen's Bridge after
Charlotte of Mecklenburgh, Wife of George III. This replaced a
former structure named Bridewell Bridge built in 1683.

The Four Courts

Father Matthew Bridge

Named after Father Theobald Matthew (1790 – 1856) the Capuchin apostle of temperance. The present bridge opened in 1818 was originally named after Charles Earl of Whitworth, the Lord Lieutenant who laid the foundation stone on 16 October 1816. There is mention of a bridge on this part of the river in 1014 and one of the public city officers cursed by Archbishop Lorcan O Tuathail in 1162 is recorded as falling to his death from the bridge. In 1210 the Normans built a new bridge here and King John on 23 August 1214 informed Archbishop Henry do Lounders that he had given the citizens permission to erect a new bridge across the Liffey and to take down the former one should they desire. This collapsed in 1385 and was rebuilt by the Dominicans in 1428. The Whitworth bridge which had four arches and was described as 'remaining a long time mouldering in decay; a blemish amidst so many fine portal edifices'. Until 1674 no other bridge crosses the Liffey.

St. Catherine's Church

ROBERT EMMET

No time was lost in carrying out the sentence of the court on the day following the trial of Robert Emmet 20 September 1803. He was taken from Kilmainham Gaol to the place of his execution, opposite St. Catherine's Church in Thomas Street. Placed on the scaffold and a rope put around his neck, Emmet was twice asked by the executioner if he was ready and answered in the negative, and before he had a chance to answer a third time, was launched into eternity. The terrors of the law were not yet complete, for after death Emmet's body was taken down and the head cut off and displayed to the crowd by the hangman Thomas Galvin with the words, 'This is the head of a traitor, Robert Emmet'.

O'Donovan Rossa Bridge

Takes its name from Jeremiah O'Donovan Rossa (1831-1915) a republican who attacked British inperialism through his paper United Ireland. Although in later years alienated from his republican colleagues he epitomised the spirit of Fenianism to a younger generation. The bridge was built in 1813 and opened in 1816 and was named Richmond Bridge after Viceroy Richmond. When sinking the foundation of the south abutment several German, Spanish and British coins were found. When the north abutment was being sunk two 18 foot long wooden boats were found, in one of which was a skeleton.

Grattan Bridge Ornaments

Grattan Bridge

Opened in 1874 and named after Henry Grattan (1746-1820) the patriot MP and orator who voted against the Act of Union but later devoted his life to the cause of Catholic emancipation. The original bridge on the site was built in 1676 and named Essex Bridge. It was the work of Sir Humphrey Jervis, one of the city's first developers. In 1687 there was severe flooding on the Liffey and part of the bridge was swept away. It was repaired and strengthened and a statue of George 1 was erected in 1722. This was removed in 1753.

Millennium Foot Bridge

Millennium Foot Bridge

Built in 2000 by Howley Harrington, architects, and Price & Myers, engineers. A delightful pedestrian bridge of remarkably gentle gradient, carried on a shallow tubular steel truss spanning from elegant swept abutments. Simple steel balustrade with bronzed aluminium handrail. The only bum note is the dirt-trapping slotted aluminium deck.

The Jennie Johnson, Famine Ship

The G.P.O. O'Connell Street

Half Penny Bridge

Built in 1816, attributed to John Windsor. The earliest recorded iron bridge in Ireland. A pedestrian toll bridge, it was built on the site of a former ferry by John Claudius Beresford and William Walsh. Three parallel elliptical cast iron ribs, each composed of six bolted sections, span between rusticated granite abutments. The bridge was cast at Coalbrookdale in Shropshire. Painted silver in the 1960's, the original off-white colour was reinstated during conservation in 2002 by Paul Arnold Architects, who also added new abutments.

O'Connell Bridge

Named after Daniel O'Connell (1775 –
1847) lawyer and politician who
opposed the Union and championed Catholic
emancipation. Built in 1794 – 98 by James Gandon and
named Carlisle Bridge after the Viceroy, it replaced a ferry
and was the lowest bridge on the river for many years. It
was widened in 1880 and the hump levelled. In 1882 it was
renamed when the statue of O'Connell was unveiled.

Rosie Hackett Bridge.

Rosie Hackett Bridge

Dublin's Newest bridge. At a cost of €13,000,000. Started in September 2011 and finished in January 2014. Is is used for public transport, taxis, bicycles, Luas and pedestrians. The builders were Graham Projects Ltd. and the engineers were Roughan & O'Donovan.

The Old Railway Hotel (The L.N.W.R.)

The boat train from Kingsbridge came along the Liffey Quays to North Wall Station and connected with the LNWR steamers. Increased traffic between the ferry and railway prompted the company to purchase a hotel just across the road from the steamer berths. In 1883 they bought the Prince of Wales Hotel at the junction of New Wapping St. and the North Wall. It opened in 1890. The immediate fate of the hotel after the LNWR ships abandoned the North Wall in 1908 is unknown, although it was still opened as a hotel the time of the 1911 census. It was occupied by British Officers during the War of independence. It became known as the British Rail Hotel after the nationalisation of the railways but ceased to be a hotel in the 1920's/ It now contains offices for Irish Rail. *By Turtle Bunbury*

Butt Bridge

Named after Isaac Butt (1813 – 79) barrister and politician, founder in 1873 of the Home Rule League. Given the freedom of the city on 4 September 1876. The present structure was built by the Dublin Port and Docks Board in 1932 and named Congress Bridge (1932 was the year of the Eucharistic Congress). It replaced a centre pivoted swing bridge, designed by Bindon Bloddy Stoney (1828 – 1909) and erected in 1879, which rarely opened to river traffic.

Talbot Memorial Bridge

Opened in 1978, Matthew Talbot (1856 – 1925).
Having taken the pledge about 1884, he became devout
and imposed severe mortifications on himself. In 1976 the
Roman Catholic Church gave him the title of 'Venerable'.
He spent his last years at no.18 Rutland Street.

Sean O'Casey Bridge

Designed by architect Cyril O'Neill and O'Connor Sutton Cronin Consulting Engineers, the bridge was built in 2005 as part of a large-scale urban renewal scheme under the Dublin Docklands Development Authority to link the north and south quays and rejuvenate both. The swing bridge spans approximately 100 metres and has two balanced cantilever arms that swing open to permit boats to pass up river. The bridge was opened by Taoiseach Bertie Ahern in July 2005. It is named for the playwright and Irish Citizens Army member Seán O'Casey (1880-1964) who lived in the North Wall area of the city.

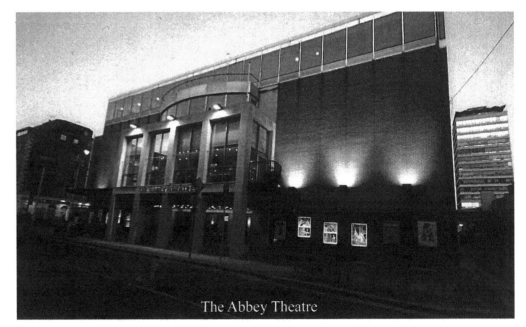

The Abbey Theatre

Samuel Beckett Bridge

Samuel Beckett Bridge

Designer by Valencian architect Santiago Calatrava and opened in 2009. The Samuel Beckett Bridge is 120 metres long, with the curved pylon 48 metres above water level. It is cable-stayed and rests on a reinforced concrete support pier which has been constructed in the River Liffey and on abutments behind the existing quay walls. It has four traffic lanes (two running north and two running south), cycle paths and footpaths and weighs 5,700 tonnes. The bridge can rotate through an angle of 90 degrees to facilitate maritime traffic.

Christ Church Cathedral

East Link Toll – Bridge

Opened in 1985, the combination of this and the Frank
Sherwin Bridge eased traffic congestion at their crossing on
the river. They afforded the facility of reversing traffic flows
on the North and South Quays with their beneficial
effects of freer movement around and access to the city.

River Liffey at Sunset

Nelson's Pillar

Left: Cork Court House; Washington Street was restored after
damage by fire during the political trials of 1891. Right: The new Church
of St. Francis in Liberty Street is built in the Byzantine style.

National Monument on Grand Parade was erected in memory of Irish patriots of the
19th century.. Right: St. Patrick's Bridge, one of the many brides spanning the River Lee.

Market, Cornmarket Street. Right: Provincial Bank, South Mall.

Left: Quay, with spire of Holy Trinity Church. Right: The School
of Commerce and Domestic Economy, Morrison's Quay.

Left: St. Fin Barre's Protestant Cathedral, from South Gate Bridge.
Right: Statues of SS. Mark, Luke, Matthew and Peter on south portal of St. Fin Barre's.

Duke of Marlborough's headquarters during the siege of 1690.
Right: The bridge and gatehouse of University College.

College, part of the National University. Left: the
attractive quadrangle. Right: the main gate.

Left: Fitzgerald Park – view of the River Lee. Right: Fitzgerald Park – children's playground.

Left: St. Mary's Roman Catholic Cathedral. Cathedral Street. The statue in front of the main entrance is of Bishop Delany..
Right: Tower of St. Ann's, Chandon. The steeple has two sides constructed of red sandstone and two of grey limestone.

Spire of the Church of the resurrection on Spangle Hill.
Right: St. Mary's Dominican Church, Pope's Quay.

Church, Summer Hill. Right: Church of the Holy Trinity, or Father Mathew
Memorial Church. The 'Apostle of Temperance' was superior here.

River Lee. Cork, second only to Dublin in population, is likewise a flourishing port. Right: Brian Bora
Drawbridge. Brian Bora was the Irish king who finally defeated the Danes in 1014 and died on the battlefield.

City Hall framed by the drawbridge. Right: Offices of the Cork Steam Packet Company, Penrose's Quay.

The Customs House and The City Hall.

River Lee. Right: Early morning, Albert Quay.

Blackrock Castle, on a promontory outside the city, was designed originally
for defensive purposes and is now a private residence.

Dublin, The Liffey. Right: The Custom House.

Lamp standards, O'Connell Bridge. Right: The width of O'Connell Bridge exceeds its length.

Some derive profit from passers-by. Right: Others derive inspiration from the river scene.

Grattan Bridge, named after the famous orator, Henry Grattan.

Boat on the River Liffey. Right: The Custom House, built by the English architect,
James Gandon, is one of the noblest buildings in Dublin.

Anything stirring down below? Right: Can't see a thing...

Custom House at night. Right: Night view of River Liffey and Eden Quay.

The east front of the Bank of Ireland. The Bank was formerly the seat of the
Irish House of Parliament. Right: The City Hall in Dame Street, formerly the Royal
Exchange, where O'Connell served as the first Catholic Mayor of Dublin.

Carved head of the Irish warrior-king Brian Boru, outside Church of Most Holy Trinity., formerly the Chapel Royal, adjoining the Castle. Right: The Genealogical Museum in Upper Castle Yard. The courtyard was called the 'Devil's Hall-Acre' because of the tortures which took place there in the rising of 1798.

The record tower of the Castle adjoins the former Chapel Royal, The Castle, built in the 13th century and twice rebuilt was the residence of the Lords Lieutenant of Ireland until 1922. Right: Christ Church Cathedral, one of the two Dublin cathedrals, both of them Protestant. It was begun by the Normans on the site of an earlier Danish church.

The Crypt of Christ Church may date back to the time of the Danish founder, Sigtryg, King of Dublin.
Right: A covered archway in Winetavern Street links Christ Church Cathedral with the Synod House.

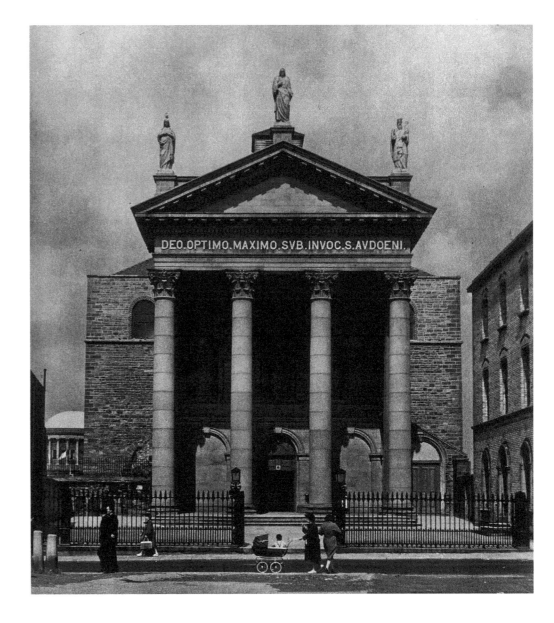

Ruins of the original St. Audoen's Church, one of the most ancient in Dublin. Right:
The modern Roman Catholic Church of St. Audoen's adjoining the earlier church.

Coopering yard, Guinness Brewery. The brewery is one of the oldest in the world and is one of Dublin's most thriving industries. Right: Modern canteen on the 600 acre site of the Guinness Brewery. The brewery is open every weekday to visitors.

Interior of St. Patrick's. The flags are of the Irish regiments and the Knights of St. Patrick.
Right: St. Patrick's. Cathedral dates from the 13th century. Jonathan Swift was Dean from 1713-1743.

The Boyle Monument in St. Patrick's was erected by Richard Boyle, Earl of Cork, to commemorate his wife and 16 children. In the foreground is a statue to Captain Boyd of H.M.S. Ajax. Right: Monuments to Ireland's illustrious men in St. Patrick's. The second on the left portrays George Nugent Temple Greville, Lord Lieutenant under Rockingham.

Sunshine and summer flowers in a Dublin street. Right: Children at play in York Street.

Mansion House, in Dawson Street, is the traditional home of Dublin's Lord Mayors. Right: The Carmelite Church of St. Teresa, off Grafton Street.

The University College, with the colleges of Cork and Galway,
constitutes part of the National University of Ireland.

The National Library, opposite the Museum, owns about half a million books and numerous manuscripts. Right:
The National Museum in Kildare Street contains a priceless collection of Irish antiquities and other treasures.

The National Gallery, next to Leinster House, is particularly noteworthy for its excellent
collection of dutch masters. Right: Leinster House, once the focal point of fashionable Dublin
life, is today the meeting place of the Dáil Éireann - the parliament of Ireland.

The College of Science, behind the Government buildings, forms part of the National University.
Right: Government buildings, Merrion Street, where all the main departments are accommodated.

A typical Georgian doorway in Merrion Street. Right: St. Andrew's Protestant Church in St. Andrew's Street.

Trinity College Library contains the priceless Book of Kells, a 7th-century illuminated copy of the Gospels. Right: Foleys Statue of Oliver Goldsmith, together with that of Edmond Burke, stands by the main entrance of Trinity Collage. Both men were students here.

Parliament Square, main quadrangle of Trinity College, with (left) the
Chapel and (right) the Campanile. Right: Trinity College Chapel.

Trinity College Examination Hall, similar in style to the Chapel. Right: Roof of Examination Hall: the organ case was captured in naval action off the coast of Spain in 1703.

Trinity College Museum: the Venetian-style entrance hall. Right: Trinity College Museum in New Square.

O'Connell Street, one of the widest thoroughfares in Europe, looking towards
O'Connell Bridge. Right: O'Connell Street in gloomier garb.

O'Connell Street: statue by Foley of Daniel O'Connell, leader of Catholic emancipation, known as the Liberator. Right: O'Connell Street: statues of William Smith O'Brien and Sir Jon Gray, the latter the founder of Dublin's water supply.

O'Connell Street: Nelson's Pillar and the General Post Office. The latter was the rebel headquarters during the Easter rising of 1916. It was destroyed by shellfire and the rebel leaders executed.

The Rotunda Hospital, oldest maternity hospital in the British Isles, designed by the German architect Cassels.

Statue of Charles Stewart Parnell, the great Irish Nationalist leader. Right: The
Rotunda assembly rooms now accommodate the celebrated Gate Theatre.

Panorama from Nelson's Pillar, showing, from left to right, the spires of St. Patrick's Cathedral, Christ Church Cathedral, Church of St. John the Baptist, and the dome of the Four Courts. Right: Marlborough Street. Nearby stood the famous Abbey Theatre, destroyed by fire in 1951.

The Presbyterian Church, Parnell Square, with its lofty spire. Right: St. George's
Church, Hardwick Crescent, one of the most elegant churches in the city.

Georgian doorway, Granby Row. Right: Church of the Holy Child, Swords Road.

The Busaras or Bus Station, the building also houses the offices of the Department of
Social Welfare. Right: Modern statuary in Marlborough Street school gardens.

Modern flats, Lower Gardiner Street. Right: Modern flats, Railway Street and Beaver Street.

The Custom House.

St. Michan's Church, dating from the 17th centry. In its vaults lie bodies which have not decayed,
owing to some preservative in the air. Right: The Four Courts, housing the central courts of justice.
This magnificent building was damaged in 1922 and restored from the original plans.

Wellington Monument in Phoenix Park, an unmistakable landmark. Right: Detail, Wellington Monument.

St. Peter's Roman Catholic Church, Phibsborough, has the highest spire in Dublin. Right: The
Royal Canal virtually defines Dublin's northern limits, as does the Grand Canal in the south.

Dublin Airport is situated at Collinstown, north of the city. The
buildings are spacious and imaginatively designed.

Howth Harbour.

Dublin Horse Show. This annual event attracts many visitors.

Dublin Hose Show., Ballbridge. The well-known horseman David Broome makes a winner's circuit.

Exhibition held during the Dublin Horse Show. Right: Dun Laoghaire, with its
fine artificial harbour, runs a regular cross-channel service with Holyhead.

HISTORY OF CORK

Cork, located on Ireland's south coast, is Ireland's second largest city and the largest city in the province of Munster. Its history dates back to the 6th century.

Origins

Cork has it beginnings in monastic settlement, founded by St Finbar in the sixth century.

However, the ancestor of the modern city was founded between 915 and 922, when Viking settlers established a trading community. The Viking leader Ottir Iarla is particularly associated with raiding and conquests in the province of Munster. The *Cogad Gáedel re Gallaib* connects this with the earliest Viking settlement of Cork. The Norse phase of Cork's history left a legacy of family names, such as Cotter and Coppinger, peculiar to Cork which are claimed to have Norse origins. In the twelfth century, this settlement was taken over by invading Anglo-Norman settlers. The Norsemen of Cork fought against the Norman incomers, mounting an expedition of 32 ships against them in 1173, which was defeated in a naval battle. Cork's city charter was granted by Prince John in 1185. Over the centuries, much of the city was rebuilt, time and again, after numerous fires. The city was at one time fully walled, and several sections and gates remain. The title of Mayor of Cork was established by royal charter in 1318, and the title was changed to Lord Mayor in 1900.

A Settler Outpost

For much of the Middle Ages, Cork city was an outpost of Old English culture in the midst of a predominantly hostile Gaelic countryside and cut off from the English government in the Pale around Dublin. Neighbouring Gaelic and Hiberno-Norman lords extorted "Black Rent" from the citizens to keep them from attacking the city. The Cork municipal government was dominated by about 12–15 merchant families, whose wealth came from overseas trade with continental Europe – in particular the export of wool and hides and the import of salt, iron and wine. Of these families, only the Ronayne family were of Gaelic Irish origin.

The medieval population of Cork was about 2,000 people. It suffered a severe blow in 1349 when almost half the townspeople died of bubonic plague when the Black Death arrived in the town. In 1491 Cork played a part in the English Wars of the Roses when Perkin Warbeck a pretender to the English throne, landed in the city and tried to recruit support for a plot to overthrow Henry VII of England. The mayor of Cork and several important citizens went with Warbeck to England but when the rebellion collapsed they were all captured and executed. Cork's nickname of the 'rebel city' originates in these events.

A description of Cork written in 1577 speaks of the city as, "the fourth city of Ireland" that is, "so encumbered with evil neighbours, the Irish outlaws, that they are fayne to watch their gates hourly...they trust not the country adjoining [and only marry within the town] so that the whole city is linked to each other in affinity".

Wars of Religion

The character of Cork was changed by the Tudor conquest of Ireland (c. 1540 – 1603) which left the English authorities in control of all of Ireland for the first time, introduced thousands of English settlers in the Plantations of Ireland and significantly, tried to impose the Protestant Reformation on a predominantly Catholic country. Cork suffered from the warfare involved in the reconquest, particularly in the Second Desmond Rebellion in 1579–83, when thousands of rural people fled to the city to avoid the fighting, bringing with them an outbreak of bubonic plague. Cork by and large sided with the Crown in these conflicts, even after a Spanish expeditionary force landed at nearby Kinsale in 1601 during the Nine Years War. However, the price the citizens demanded for their loyalty was toleration of their Roman Catholic religion. In 1603, the citizens of Cork along with Waterford and Limerick rebelled, expelling Protestant ministers, imprisoning English officials, seizing the municipal arsenals and demanding freedom of worship for Catholics. They refused to admit Lord Mountjoy's English army when it marched south, citing their charters from 12th century. Mountjoy retorted that he would, "cut King John his charter with King James his sword" and arrested the ringleaders, thus ending the revolt. It was an ominous sign for the coming century. In 1641, Ireland was convulsed by the Irish Rebellion of 1641. Cork became a stronghold for the English Protestants, who sought refuge there after the outbreak of the rebellion and remained in Protestant hands throughout the ensuing Irish Confederate Wars. An ineffective Irish Confederate attempt to take the city in 1642 was beaten off at the battle of Liscarroll. In 1644, Murrough O'Brien, Earl Inchiquinn, the commander of English forces in Cork, expelled the Catholic townsmen from city. Although most of them went no further than the city's suburbs, this was the beginning of Protestant domination of the city that would last for nearly two centuries. The population of Cork by this times was around 5000, most of whom lived outside the city walls.

In 1649–53, Ireland was re-conquered by an English Parliamentarian army under Oliver Cromwell. Inchiquin had briefly led Cork into an alliance with the Confederates, in 1648, but the garrison changed sides again in 1650, going over to English Parliamentarian side under the influence of Roger Boyle, 1st Earl of Orrery.

In 1690 during the Williamite war in Ireland, Cork was besieged and taken for the Williamites by an English army under John Churchill, 1st Duke of Marlborough.

Eighteenth Century Cork

In the late 17th and early 18th centuries French Protestants (Huguenots) arrived in Cork fleeing from religious persecution at the hands of Louis XIV of France. Their influence can still be seen in the names of the Huguenot Quarter and French Church Street. Many new buildings were erected in Cork in the 18th century. Like Dublin, much of Cork's medieval architecture was replaced by neo-classical Georgian buildings. Examples of this include, Christ Church (1720–26), St Anne's Shandon (1722–26) and a Customs House (1724). During the 18th century, trade in Cork's port expanded considerably. Cork merchants exported large amounts of butter and beef to Britain, the rest of Europe and North America.

Population Explosion, Famine and Emigration

During the early 19th century the population of Cork expanded rapidly. By mid-century Cork had a population of about 80,000. The increase was due to migration from the countryside as people fled from poverty and in the 1840s, a terrible famine. This led to extremes of poverty and overcrowding in Cork city during this century. Another effect of this influx was to reverse the denominational character of the city, which became predominantly Catholic again.

However, in the later 19th century the population of Cork declined slightly due to emigration, principally to Britain or North America. In 1825, over 1,800 Irish residents departed from Cork to emigrate to Peterborough, Ontario, Canada assisted by Peter Robinson (who organised the scheme on behalf of the British Government). This resulted in the area known as "Scott's Plains" being renamed "Peterborough" as a tribute. Cork and also nearby Cobh became major points of departure for Irish emigrants, who left the country in great numbers after the Great Irish Famine of the 1840s.

During the 19th and early 20th century important industries in Cork included, brewing, distilling, wool and shipbuilding. In addition, there were some municipal improvements such as gas light street lights in 1825, two local papers, the Cork Constitution published from 1823 and the Cork Examiner, first published in 1841 and, very importantly for the development of modern industry, the railway reached Cork in 1849. Also in 1849, University College Cork opened.

Much 19th century architecture can still be seen in many areas around the city such as the neo- Georgian and Victorian buildings that now house Banks and Department stores. The Victorian influence on the city is noticeable in place names such as Victoria Cross (after Queen Victoria), Albert Quay (after Prince Albert), Adelaide Street (after Queen Adelaide) and the Victoria Hospital on the Old Blackrock Rd.

Since the nineteenth century, Cork had been a strongly Irish nationalist city, with widespread support for Irish Home Rule and the Irish Parliamentary Party, but from 1910 stood firmly behind William O'Brien's dissident All-for-Ireland Party. O'Brien published a third local newspaper, the Cork Free Press.

Tans, Troubles and Civil War

Following the outbreak of World War I in 1914 many of Cork's National Volunteers enlisted to served with the Royal Munster Fusiliers, suffering heavy casualties both in Gallipoli and on the Western Front. In the period 1916–1923, Cork was embroiled in a conflict between radical Irish nationalists and the British state in Ireland. The turmoil of this period ultimately led to substantial Irish independence for 26 of the 32 Irish counties in 1922, but also to a bitter civil war between Irish nationalist factions in 1922–23.

In 1916, during the Easter Rising as many as 1000 Irish Volunteers mobilised in Cork for an armed rebellion against British rule but they dispersed without fighting. However, during the subsequent Irish War of Independence 1919–1921, Cork was the scene of much violence.

In particular, the city suffered from the action of the Black and Tans – a paramilitary police force raised to help the Royal Irish Constabulary combat the Irish Republican Army. On 20 March 1920, Thomas Mac Curtain, the Sinn Féin Lord Mayor of Cork was shot dead, in front of his wife at his home, by Policemen. His successor as Mayor, Terence McSwiney was arrested in August 1920 and died on hunger strike in October of that year. On 11 December the city centre was gutted by fires started by the Black and Tans in reprisal for IRA attacks in the city. Over 300 buildings were destroyed and two suspected IRA men were shot dead in their beds by British forces on the night. This atrocity did not stop IRA activity in the city however.

Attacks and reprisals continued in the city until the fighting was ended in a truce agreed in July 1921.

Another, highly disputed aspect of the War of Independence in Cork was the shooting of informers. Historians such as Peter Hart have written that 'enemy' groups such as Protestants and ex-soldiers were targeted at random by the IRA. Gerard Murphy's "Year of the Disappearances, (2010) put the number of Protestants killed in Cork at 73. This thesis is disputed by other scholars such as John Borgonovo, who write that their studies suggest that the IRA's 30 or so confirmed civilian victims in Cork do seem to have been targeted because the IRA believed they were passing information to the British and not for any other reason.

Civil War

The local IRA units, for the most part, did not accept the Anglo-Irish Treaty negotiated to end the war -ultimately repudiating the authority of the newly created Irish Free State. After the withdrawal of British troops in early 1922, they took over the military barracks in Cork and the surrounding area. By July 1922, when the Irish Civil War, broke out, Cork was held by anti-Treaty forces as part of a self-styled Munster Republic -intended to be a stronghold for the preservation of the Irish Republic annulled by the Treaty.

Cork however, was taken in August 1922 by the pro-Treaty National Army in an attack from the sea. The Free State forces landed at nearby Passage West with 450 troops and several artillery pieces. There was fighting for three days in the hills around Douglas and Rochestown, in which roughly 20 men were killed and about 60 wounded as the anti-Treaty IRA contested the National Army's advance into the city. However the badly armed anti-Treaty forces did not make a stand in Cork itself and dispersed after sporadic fighting, burning a number of buildings and the barracks they had been holding (for example at Elizabeth Fort and Collins Barracks).

Subsequently they reverted to guerrilla warfare and took to destroying all the roads and bridges connecting Cork with the rest of the country. Michael Collins, commander in chief of the National Army, was killed in an IRA ambush at Beal na mBlath, west of the city on 25 August 1922.

Guerrilla warfare raged in the surrounding countryside until April 1923, when the Anti-Treaty side called a ceasefire and dumped their arms. There were attacks on Free State troops in the city, but not on the scale of the campaign against British forces in 1919–21.

Late Twentieth Century Cork

In the post-independence period, Cork has been acknowledged as the Republic of Ireland's second city. It has produced a number of political leaders, notably Jack Lynch – who became Taoiseach (Irish prime minister) in the 1960s. Its citizens half jokingly refer to it as the "real capital".

Cork's inner city slums were cleared by the municipal authority from the 1920s onwards, and their inhabitants were re-housed in housing estates on the periphery of the city -especially on its north side. Many of these new suburbs have since suffered from social deprivation and high crime rates – a pattern repeatedly found in Irish urban development.

Cork's economy dipped in the late 20th century as the old manufacturing industries in Cork declined. The Ford car factory closed in 1984 as did the Dunlop tyre factory. Shipbuilding in Cork also came to an end in the 1980s. As a result of these closures unemployment was high in Cork in the 1980s.

However, in the 1990s new industries came to Cork. For instance, Marina Commercial Park was built on the site of the old Dunlop and Ford plants and Cork Airport Business Park first opened in 1999. Cork, like other cities in Ireland benefited somewhat from the Celtic Tiger economic boom, with growth in industries such as information technology, chemicals, brewing, distilling and food processing. The Port of Cork is also a busy and important port.

Into the 21st century, tourism has grown in economic importance, and in 2005 Cork was named European Capital of Culture.

St. Patrick's Bridge

Barryscourt Castle.

Thomas Davis Bridge

Prior to 1824 and about this time, the suburb of Sunday's Well was also developing. The nearest river crossing for the residents to gain access to the city was the North Gate bridge, and in order to make life easier, it was decided to build the bridge that today is named Thomas Davis Bridge.

On completion the bridge was named wellington Bridge, later it was changed to Thomas Davis Bridge that very many people still refer to by its original name. A plaque on the wall states that the name change was by decree of the Corporation Thomas Davis having been born in Mallow in 1814, dedicated his life to the cause of Ireland and died in Dublin in 1845

Daly's Bridge

Daly's Bridge

Daly's Bridge is a pedestrian bridge spanning the river Lee in Cork. Known locally as the Shakey bridge, it joins Sunday's Well road on the northside to Fitzgerald's Park in the south. Completed in 1926 and opened in 1927, it is the only suspension bridge in Cork City and was constructed by the London based David Rowell & Company. Constructed primarily of wrought iron, the bridge spans 160 feet and the timber planked walkway is four and a half feet wide. The bridge takes its official name from Cork businessman James Daly who contributed to the cost of the bridge. It's colloquial name (the 'Shakey Bridge') derives from the movement of the platform when running or jumping on the bridge.

The Bounty on a visit to Cork Harbour

The Bounty was built in 1960 in Lunenburg,Nova Scotia from the keel up by the shipwrights, of Smith and Rhuland Shipyard,following the original plans in the British Naval maritime Museum. Metro-Goldwyn-Meyer studios commissioned the ship to be built at a cost of $750,000 to star in the 1962 film 'Mutiny on the Bounty' with Marlon Brando and Trever Howard Work began in February of 1960 and on August 27 of that year the ship set sail for Tahiti to begin primary filming.
SADLY THE BOUNTY SANK IN A STORM IN 2011 WITH THE LOSS OF TWO LIVES

Mardyke Bridge

On Monday 28th February 2005 a new bridge to facilitate connection
between the western end of the Distillery grounds and the Mardyke on the other side. The project was undertaken with the active partnership of UCC who gained a
cross-river access from the main campus to their music department at Sundays Well.

Blackrock Castle

The rocky limestone outcrop on which Blackrock Castle sits today has been a site of fortification since the late sixteenth century. The tower was built in 1582 to protect the city from pirates and raiders and also acted as a sentinel to guide shipping safely to and from the port. The castle now houses an observatory, restaurant, bar and an award winning state-of-the-art science exhibition

Distillery Gate Bridge

Distillery Gate Bridge

Otherwise known as Wyse's (Wyse's distillery is located here)
or Reilly's named after Reilly's marsh which is near by.

Queens Old Castle, Daunt Square

For well over 100 years, it was one of the best-known shops in Cork City.
Currently home to retails such as Argos and formerly Virgin Megastore.

St. Vincent's Bridge

During the bad flooding in 2009 there was considerable damage caused to the quay walls very close to the bridge. There were worries concerning the stability of this bridge at that time. This current bridge dates from 1878 and it is the second bridge to be built on this site. It serves here as a footbridge over the North channel, leading to the Sundays Well District.

Fota House

This was originally a modest 2 storey hunting lodge belonging to the Smith Barry family. In the 1820's the family had it converted into an elegant residence.
The house has over 17 rooms and since its re-opening in 2009 after restoration,
People can now visit its upper floors for the first time in many years.

Griffith Bridge (North Gate Bridge)

Griffith Bridge is located on an ancient gate site into the northern side of Corks
Medieval city half a mile to the west of St. Patrick's bridge. Many different bridges have been placed in this location
over the years. The iron structure was replaced in 1961 by the present bridge. It is named after Arthur Griffith an
Irish patriot and leader of the 1916 Easter Rising but is commonly referred to as North Gate bridge.

Cork Bank, Parnell Place

The Cork Savings bank was also built in the 1800s, designed by the Kearne Bros., and Sir Thomas Deane.

Shandon Bridge

Shandon Bridge is another relative newcomer. Built only in 2004 as a
pedestrian link between Shandon and Shandon Street and the heart of the City.

St. Anne's, Shandon

The Church of St. Anne's is one of Cork's oldest building. Built in 1722 it's almost 300 years old. The famous 8 bells in the tower were cast by Rudhalls of Gloucester in 1750. They weigh over 6 tonnes and each bear an original inscription

Christy Ring Bridge

The Christy Ring bridge was opened on Friday 13th February 1987 by Lord Mayor Gerry O'Sulivan
in the presence of Christy's family. The bridge was built by Ascon and cost nearly seven million euros.

CHRISTY RING

Nicholas Christopher Michael Ring (12 October 1920[2] - 2 March 1979), better known as Christy Ring, was a famous Irish sportsperson. He played hurling with the Glen Rovers club from 1941 until 1967 and was a member of the Cork senior inter-county team from 1939 until 1963. Ring is widely regarded as one of the greatest hurlers in the history of the game. Many former players, commentators and fans rate him as the number one player of all-time.

Metropole Hotel, MacCurtain Street

The Metropole was designed by architect Arthur Hill and built to the highest standards. Not only did the Metropole incorporate the height of late nineteenth century luxury, it also had one other feature. In keeping with Musgrave Bros' refusal to deal in alcohol the Metropole was a temperance or "dry" hotel.

St. Patrick's Bridge

St. Patrick's Bridge

The first bridge was built here in 1789 and it was for some time a toll bridge. The opening ceremony for this current bridge was held in 1861. St. Patrick's Bridge flows across the river from the main street of the city - St. Patrick's Street. It leads on to Bridge Street and connections to the city's' Northside along with routes to Dublin and the East.

Brian Boru Bridge

This was one of two 'Railway bridges'. Trains ran across the river using tracks
on the bridge and on its mirror image - Clontarf Bridge. It could raise up to allow river traffic to pass.

GRAND PARADE. CORK. 1922.W.L.

Grand Parade, Cork

The Grand Parade is the widest street in Cork, built over a channel of the river Lee. It is among the most important archaeological
sites in Cork. It is near to the earliest sites inhabited by the Hiberno-Norse settlers. Among the items found
during excavation were pottery, nails and wooden structures from houses. Many
of the finds are on display at the Cork Public Museum.

Michael Collins Bridge

Opened in 1984 and named after the former General of the Irish Republican army Michael Collins. Along with Eamonn De Valera bridge it is the further most down-stream bridge in the city at present. There are plans to develop another bridge downstream from here but that will span the river after the channels have rejoined. On the occasion of the opening of both bridges in 1984, descendants of both families were present.

MICHAEL COLLINS

Michael Collins (16 October 1890 – 22 August 1922) was an Irish revolutionary leader, Minister for Finance and Teachta Dála (TD) for Cork South in the First Dáil of 1919, Director of Intelligence for the IRA, and member of the Irish delegation during the Anglo-Irish Treaty negotiations. Subsequently, he was both Chairman of the Provisional Government and Commander-in-chief of the National Army.[2] Throughout this time, at least as of 1919, he was also President of the Irish Republican Brotherhood, and, therefore, under the bylaws of the Brotherhood, President of the Irish Republic. Collins was assassinated in August 1922 during the Irish Civil War.

Imperial Hotel, South Mall, Cork

The hotel was first open in 1816 around the time of Napoleon and Wellington.
Designed by young Cork architect Thomas Deane, the dignified facade remains virtually unchanged
toady and forms the front portion and main entrance of the Imperial Hotel.

Eamonn De Valera Bridge

Eamonn De Valera Bridge was opened in 1984 and was built as part of a ring-road traffic development plan formulated in the 1970's and known as the Land Utilisation and Transportation system or the LUTS plan. Both this bridge and the Michael Collins Bridge, the other of the pair, were built by Ascon Ltd.

EAMONN DE VALERA

Éamon de Valera (14 October 1882 – 29 August 1975) was one of the dominant political figures in twentieth-century Ireland. His political career spanned over half a century, from 1917 to 1973; he served multiple terms as head of government and head of state. He also led the introduction of the Constitution of Ireland. De Valera was a leader of Ireland's struggle for independence from Britain in the War of Independence and of the anti-Treaty opposition in the ensuing Irish Civil War (1922–1923). In 1926, he founded Fianna Fáil, and was head of government (President of the Executive Council, later Taoiseach) from 1932 to 1948, 1951 to 1954, and 1957 to 1959, when he resigned after being elected as President
of Ireland. His political creed evolved from militant republicanism to social and cultural conservatism.[4]

Victoria Hotel, Patrick's Street, Cork

built in 1810 and retains much of its Victorian splendour. The hotel was frequented by European royalty and leading Irish politicians.
In the literary world James Joyce recounts his stay here in his novel '*A Portrait of the Artist as a Young Man*'

Clontarf Bridge

Clontarf Bridge is one of a pair of railway bridges that were opened on new year's day 1912 and were designed to connect the railway terminus of the Great Southern and Western Railway at Glanmire Road to the north of here with train services that ran south and west of the city and which had their termini to the south of the river. These were both built as Scherzer Rollin Lift Bascule Bridges, which meant that they opened through the use of counter-weights, to allow access to shipping. Rail traffic operated on the bridge until the 1970's after which they were re-conformed just for traffic and pedestrians usage.

Coliseum, MacCurtain Street, Cork

Originally one of Cork's iconic Cinemas, was opened in 1913 remained in use until the 1970s. It is now home to the Leisureplex bowling alley.

Parnell Bridge

PARNELL BRIDGE CORK. 2604. W.L.

Parnell Bridge

Named in Honour of the 'Uncrowned King of Ireland', Charles Stewart Parnell, the bridge was built in the early 1830's to facilitate access to the Corn Market on Sleigh's Marsh. Located where the City Hall is today, just to the South. This first bridge was named Angleasa bridge and had a movable centre section to facilitate shipping through it. This was replaced in 1882 with the first Parnel Bridge, which again had a shipping access facility. When this bridge was deemed unsafe in 1968 the new fixed structure was built and opened in 1971 by Lord Mayor Peter Barry

Parliament Bridge

The first bridge at this site was built in 1764 but the one that stands here today was built in 1806. It suffered damage in an explosion during the war of independence and needed further repairs in the early 1930's. The bridge was completely re-strengthened during the 1990's to cater for massively increased traffic flows.

Trinity Bridge

As you approach the Bridge you cannot help but notice the spire of Holy Trinity Church - also known as Fr. Mathew's Church. It was from here that he served for many years, ministering to Cork's poor in the 1830's and during the famine years. Form here also he spread the gospel of temperance in his great national crusade of the 1840's. Trinity Bridge was opened in 1977 by Lord Mayor Gerard Goldberg. Gerard Goldberg was of Lithuanian Jewish heritage and served with distinction as Cork's first citizen in that year. The bridge is unusual in that it was paid for entirely from the proceeds of the newly introduced parking discs in the city.

South Gate Bridge

This is the oldest bridge over the River Lee. Most lively a bridge has been at this site since the time of the Vikings arrival in Cork. The north sides of the bridge were occupied by the South Gate Prison. The heads of executed criminals were displayed on spikes here during the sixteenth and seventeenth centuries.

Nano Nagle Bridge

This is the only bridge named after a woman in the city and was built as part of a number of infrastructural developments to celebrate the Cork 800 years in 1985. Nano Nagle was born at Ballygriffing, Co. Cork in 1718, during penal times. Despite the repression of those years, concerned at the plight of young Catholic girls in the city, she founded her first school in 1754. To continue her work she founded the Presentation Order of nuns in 1775 and she also set up the South Presentation Convent at 50 Cove Street.

Nano Nagle died on 26 April 1784

Clarkes Bridge

Second oldest bridge over the Lee was built in 1726, of red clay-slate. Known in the past as 'Wandesford Bridge' it used to provide access to the famous Cork Waterloo Glass factory. Now connects Wandesford Quay with Hanover Street.

St. Finbarre's Bridge

Dating from 1999 this bridge links Cork's Western Road with Sharman Crawford Street. Cork's Lord Mayor, Cllr. Damien Wallace, on opening the bridge, suggested that the bridge would open up a new era for the South Parish, one of Cork's oldest communities.

Eye, Ear & Throat Hospital, Cork

The Cork Ophthalmic Hospital was founded in October 1868 in Nile Street (Sheares Street). In 1897 the Hospital was opened on the Western Road and patients were transferred from Nile Street to the present building.

Lancaster Bridge

Lancaster Bridge

A new bridge over the river was required for access to the new hotel at Lancaster Quay mixed use development in the city centre of Cork. Constructed between December 2005 to March 2006.

O'Donovan's Bridge

Opened in 1902. Built to provide access to the then newly developed 'Fernhurst' housing area.

Gaol Bridge

Dates from 1835. Limestone built and designed by Brunel.

University Bridge

University Bridge

Opened in 1929 leads from Western Road into University College Cork.

O'Neill Crowley Bridge

Completed in 1820. Three arches span a fifty one foot crossing of the Lee connecting to Western Road. Formerly George IV Bridge it is one and a half miles west from the Grand Parade. Peter O'Neill Crowley is also Commemorated at the National Monument on the Grand Parade in Cork which was unveiled on St. Patrick's Day 1906.

National Monument, Grand Parade

Sailing On The river Lee

Waterworks On The River Lee

Christ Church, South Main Street

Patrick Street, Cork, in the 1920s.
Right: Longshoreman sculpture, Dublin, River Liffey.

Clockwise from bottom left: St. Mary's Cathedral, Cork; iconic building on Lavitts Quay, Cork; The Capital cinema Cork; the Jameson Distillery, Middleton, Co.Cork. The Distillery at Middleton.

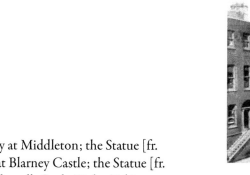

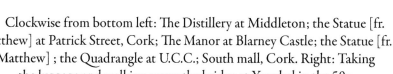

Clockwise from bottom left: The Distillery at Middleton; the Statue [fr. Matthew] at Patrick Street, Cork; The Manor at Blarney Castle; the Statue [fr. Matthew] ; the Quadrangle at U.C.C.; South mall, Cork. Right: Taking the luggage and walking across the bridge at Youghal in the 50s.

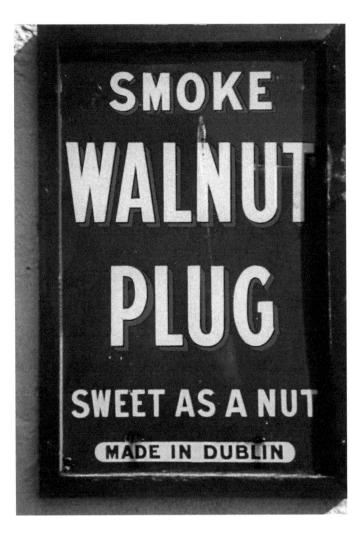

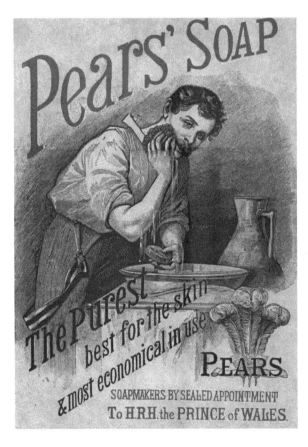

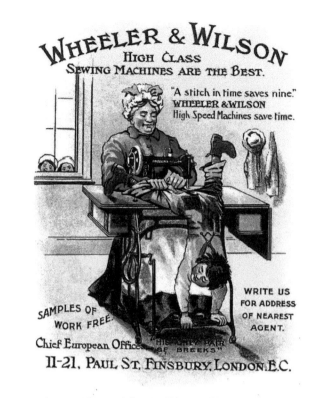

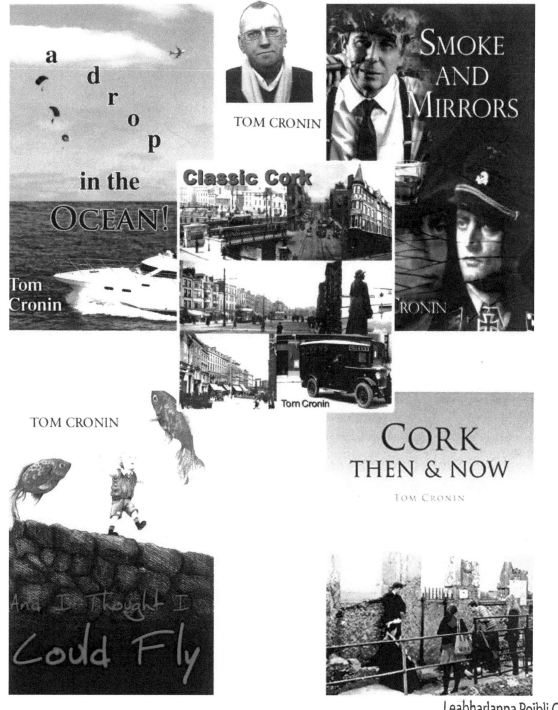